Thanksgiving in Vegas

Thanksgiving in Vegas

Curt Johnson

december press

Bottlehouse Books

A special issue of **December Magazine**,
comprising vol. 38, no. 3, 1995

Thanksgiving in Vegas by Curt Johnson

ISBN: 0-913204-31-1
Library of Congress Catalog Card Number: 95-67093

Manufactured in the United States of America

Part I of this book appeared in ARX Magazine, March 1970, in slightly different form as "Love from Shirley Temple."

Published by December Press
Box 302 Highland Park, Illinois 60035
and Bottlehouse Books,
Box 43 Bishop Hill, Illinois 61419
Book design & digital typography by R. Lane.

For Necia —

A day of sunlight and swallows…
And saw the fireman, by the fiddley, wave.
And laughed. And went on digging my own grave.

— Malcolm Lowry

I

He turned the key carefully and then he brought his fist down hard above the lock and the catch opened and the trunk's lid sprang up. "You want me to change it for you?" he asked, and she laughed — a quick, low, laugh, pulling her head back slightly, and he grinned at her.

When he had finished he put the flat and the tools and her luggage back into the trunk, but when he reached for the lid she put her hand on his arm. "I'll keep this," she said. She lifted a small, green bag out of the trunk and took a pocket flask from it. "If you don't mind sharing," she said and sipped once from the flask before handing it to him. When he put his head back to swallow he could see the underside of a reef of clouds reflecting the lights of a town ahead and he thought — the sailor's dream.

She drove through the town and out of it before she finally spoke again, turning her head to look at him. "I'm Barbara, uh…. Barbara Mitchell." She smiled as she gave her last name and he could see her teeth glisten in the light from the dash. Her eyes were only half open, as if she were tired from driving all day, maybe.

"I'm Barry Terveer," he said. "Do you live out here — in Los Angeles?"

She turned her head to look at him. "No. I'm from New York. One of the things my father is always warning me against is hitchhikers. He's very protective."

"Yuh." He waited a moment then before he said, "I guess it's not such a good idea. Not for a lone woman."

"He told me especially to avoid servicemen…. Look, would you be willing to do me still another favor? I have to see someone up in the hills about 20 miles from here. Do you have enough time?"

She didn't speak again until they were almost there.

"How old are you?" she asked then and he told her he was 19.

"You look older," she said. "I have almost eight years on you. You're from the Midwest, aren't you?"

They backtracked only once on the winding hill roads before she found the house. It was high up, under tall, bare-trunked trees near a turnaround at the end of the road. The path to it went through an overhang of bushes that brushed his face as he followed her. She put her small bag under her arm and knocked once and almost immediately the door was opened. "Come in, Barbara," a tall, red-faced man said warmly, "you're a little late." The man was wearing tight yellow pants and a faded, green, Marine-surplus undershirt and he was barefooted and bald, and there was a square of white bandage taped across the center of his forehead. "And this is…?"

"This is a friend of mine, Mr. Hobson. Barry Trevor."

"Terveer," Barry said, and shook the man's large hand.

They entered and the man padded past them to the far end of the kitchen and took three water glasses from a shelf above the sink and poured them full from a gallon of red wine. "Never knew a white hat to turn down a snort," he said, and chuckled. "Or anything else."

When he handed the woman's glass to her he said, "You ready to do business?" His face had deep creases in it and the bottom half was ringed with a fringe of red beard.

They stood there a moment, holding their glasses of wine, and then the woman shrugged and turned and went through a narrow door into the next room and they followed her. The kitchen, a bathroom off it, and this room were the entire house. This room had only one dim lamp in it, on a stand in the corner next to the headboard of an oversize bed; that, and half a dozen strings of colored Christmas-tree bulbs taped along the ceiling, their lights blinking slowly on and off.

"Well, Barbara," the man said warmly, softly, going to the bed, "I'm glad you're here, late or not." He eased himself down, his legs stretching out toward a film projector at the foot of the bed.

Barbara seated herself in the only chair in the room and now she placed the green bag in her lap. "I brought what you agreed to — with Richard," she said.

Barry rested the back of his thighs against a long table and sipped at his wine. The door at the end of the room was covered with photos of nude women; a square of white paper was taped at the door's center, the projector on the bed pointing out at it.

"A little editing, friend," Hobson said, raising his voice. "Can I offer you a little Mexican love weed? Speak up, swab jockey."

Barry made his expression blank, impassive, and stared back at the man.

"I think if — " the woman began but Hobson was pushing himself away from the headboard. "No offense, sailor," he said. His voice was still soft. "But you know, Barbara and I, we have a bit of business to transact, and...." His smile broadened and Arnie looked at the woman; she nodded at him and smiled, a bored smile. "If you like," Hobson said, "why don't you go pour yourself another."

In the kitchen Barry poured himself a second glass of wine, sipping it, hoping that whatever transaction was taking place would be quickly finished because he wanted one good shot at Barbara Mitchell and then if nothing worked out — why, then, he might still be able to get back to the base in time. He turned his head and spat twice into the sink, wishing he had gone back with the rest from Frisco and taken the short trip to Tijuana, and then he spat a third time for luck, and washed the red stain into the drain with a jet from the faucet.

He saw a framed photograph on the top of the refrigerator, at the back, under a cupboard, and he went to it and pulled it forward: a photo of Shirley Temple, nine or ten years old maybe, smiling out brightly, all dimples and sparkling eyes and blonde ringlets. He inspected the inscription on the photo: "LOVE FROM...," the handprinting following the curved white stripes of Shirley's collar, the large penciled letters like those a child would make.

He went to the sink and poured himself a third glass of the sweet red wine, and then he went back through the narrow door into the room.

"...tent in back's still there," Hobson was saying as he entered "but my baby's done gone and left me and I'm afraid I've nothing to offer by way of quid pro quo." He stopped and looked from the woman's face to Barry's. "Everything all right, sailor? No hard feelings?" He chuckled. "Maybe you'd like to see one of my films, long as you're here?"

"No. No thanks," Barry said. He glanced at the woman and she shook her head once quickly. "I meant to ask you," he said then, "what happened to your head?"

"*This?*" Hobson's voice rose sharply. "Lousy pachucos jumped me, that's what happened." His voice dropped back to its soft, gentle tone. "Broke one of the greaser's jaws, though. Must of got lucky."

"Mr. Hobson," the woman said, sitting slightly forward in her chair now, "are we agreed then or not? I've told you I have very little influence with my father. Send him some samples, if you like, but what he does at the magazine — "

Quietly but firmly Hobson interrupted her. "If he doesn't pay any attention to you, why should — ?"

"Look — I'm willing to give you what you and Richard agreed was fair, as long as that's an end to it. I can't influence my father and what you seem to be suggesting now is out of the question."

"What's your opinion, young fella?" Hobson said. "Would you — ?"

"I don't know what it's all about," Barry said, interrupting the other easy because Hobson had come on soft himself most of the time and those were usually the worst because if you got them upset they could turn all the way around. "It sounds to me, though, like it's no deal — whatever deal it was supposed to be."

"Fine. Fine with me. It's her funeral. Maybe she'll change her mind… and maybe she won't. But either way, I'll get what's coming to me, one way or another. When should I expect to hear from you again then — Miss Barbara?"

"You won't. You'll hear from Richard." She looked back at the man with a half-smile on her lips, her eyes almost closed. Calm, Barry thought, she gives that impression almost; cool.

Hobson had pushed himself away from the headboard. "Richard!" he said scornfully, "I wait for King Scarfer, I'll starve." He was standing now. "I promise you, I'll do what I have to!"

The woman was at the narrow door and because he wanted to give her time to get out of the house and to the car, Barry said, "Is that Shirley Temple's writing? On the photograph?"

"Where?" Hobson said loudly. He padded quickly around the bed to Barry. "In the kitchen? You bet it is. Used to turn out a couple thousand of those a month. For her agent. So he had her write on one for me. When she made *Wee Willie Winkie*." He looked away from Barry's face and then back again. "You know,

you and me, we could have had us a good thing here tonight —
with your little lady friend. Still can. What do you say?" he was
standing a foot from Barry now and under the changing ceiling
lights his fringe of beard and the creased skin of his face were
shifting colors. "Unbutton some of those 13 buttons."

"Well," Barry said, suddenly tired of waiting, "I say you're just
another California loony, Jack. But thanks for the vino — anyway."

"Oh," the man said softly. "Oh. Well, sure. Okay, swabbie. No
sweat." His voice dropped very low. "But you tell her she's got till
Wednesday. I like you, friend. Tell you what — tell her she can
bring you along and Richard's frau. You tell Miss High and
Mighty Radcliffe that, hear me?"

Barry turned from the man.

"Hear me, deck ape? Or maybe it's black gang."

"Yuh," Barry said, walking toward the door. "I hear you." He
was trying to put together an approach that would guarantee
success with a woman of experience and cool.

◆

Barry drove the car away from Hobson's, down the hill and
then south on the highway toward Los Angeles, both of them
silent until she asked him wasn't he tired? didn't he need sleep
too? because she certainly did.

He carried her bags to the desk, then he carried them to their
rooms, feeling that she was exacting advance payment for what
was to come, but not especially resentful about it, too excited for
that by the thought of what was to come, by the swing of her skirt
ahead of him very different, all of her, from what he was used to
and when the bottle of scotch and the ice she had ordered arrived
they each had a drink and then she opened the door between their
rooms and asked him if he didn't want to wash up before their
food arrived. The desk clerk had called out to a Chinese restaurant for her.

He took his duffle bag to his room and in about ten minutes
she came in holding two fresh drinks. She was wearing some kind
of short, loose dressing gown now — light orange in color, some
kind of black pattern to it — and her lips were bare of lipstick and
her black hair hung loose to her shoulders and she was barefooted.
She sat down on the bed beside him, looked at him, laughed a low,

5

quiet laugh, said, "Well, here we are." When he took his drink from her he held her wrist a moment to look at her watch. "Two o'clock," he said. "So it's all right to kiss me — I'm AWOL in six hours."

"Oh, you're not," she said. "I'm sorry." She leaned to him and gave him a quick, dry kiss on the side of his forehead. "I'm sorry — is it serious?"

"No. I go up for discharge in three weeks. It's too late for them to do much now, except restriction."

She started to talk about herself — she was on vacation and she had these friends near Hollywood and she had been wondering if he would have any interest in meeting them. But since he had to get back, well — and then the Chinese food arrived.

"I wish they'd sent along fortune cookies," she said, tearing open the wrapper on a pair of chopsticks. She dished for them from the white paper boxes.

When they had finished he asked her if she wanted more scotch and got up and made them two strong drinks.

"…it has to be in three parts." She was telling him now about her undergraduate thesis. "And it has to be exactly 40 pages long — exactly, including footnotes." She shook her head, smiled at him. "I wrote on Hawthorne's 'My Kinsman.' Have you read that?"

He sipped his drink, watched her. No, Jesus Christ, lady, he thought, I haven't read that.

She took a deep breath and arched her back and relaxed again. "I discovered a Theseus motif in it, in 'Kinsman.' The echoes of it. They thought it was so good they wanted me to expand it into a doctoral dissertation." She yawned, put her fingertips to her mouth. "But I took a job in New York instead. My father… well, never mind. But I have my own apartment. I have to. They're too possessive to live with, really — my family. So many ties. So complicated. But — "

He started pacing slowly around the room as she talked — becoming very aware of the bed each time he passed it — and finally he interrupted. "Barbara, how bad are you in trouble with that crackpot?"

"Hobson? Nothing I can't handle. Chiefly because he's so stupid. Wasn't that your impression of him? My god, *editing* stag movies!"

"He said to tell you he wants to hear from you by Wednesday."

"All right, you've told me. He'll hear from me — personally." She set her glass on the table and stood up and came to him. "Look — we're both tired so why don't we get some sleep?"

"You mean let's go to bed?"

She shook her head and he put one arm around her, the other holding his drink away from them, and kissed her, urging her toward the bed with his arm. But then she held him away. "There," she said, "that's all."

"We could stay awake until it gets light enough to see to drive to your friends. Beats sleeping, honest to God it does."

"Not tonight."

For a moment he considered making it a contest of wills or of strength alone, but then he decided not even to try because, for one thing, he was so tired he would only get angry.

She stood up from the bed. She pointed at the bottle. "You keep it," she said. "You can drown your sorrows if you want to. I'm going to bed."

He heard the catch on her side of the door between their rooms snap shut.

◆

Barbara met him outside the mansion, sitting on a long plank bench and wearing a long, white, ruffled dress. He went to her and raised her by the hands to kiss her but as he put his arms around her she spoke to someone behind him: "Look — what did I tell you," and he turned, and there was her husband and another man, the two dressed in hunting clothes, shotguns cradled across their arms.

They gave him a 10-minute start — he remembered how desperate he felt when her husband spoke, and how calm Barbara's expression was — and even though he did not remember being caught, or even being chased in his dream, he knew they had trapped him and killed him, because just before the phone woke him a Negro boy was being taken down the plantation's dusty road in a slat wagon — to town and the gallows — the boy's Mammy with him, comforting him, singing — the Negro boy because Barbara's husband had forced the boy to make a false confession, and that was when the phone woke him.

He showered and brushed his blues down and dressed and was ready when she knocked at the door. He had decided to give up and ask her for a ride to the other side of L.A. But when she knocked he remembered the bottle and went to the stand beside his bed to get it and it was gone. And he did remember putting it there before he fell asleep.

They went down to the motel's pool and took lounge chairs beside it and ordered eggs and bacon and toast and coffee — a pitcher of orange juice to start. "If you carried gin in your flask," he said, "we could have a screwdriver to start the day. Do you have your flask in your bag?" She shook her head once and gave him a polite half-smile, but she was wearing sunglasses and he could not read her eyes. In the sunlight her black hair had a blue cast to it.

"I wish we were going north," she said. "We could go wine-tasting together. And we could see San Francisco at night together. Don't you ever get the urge just to *leave*? Give up all your ties?"

"Yes. Only I don't have any ties except to Uncle Sam — and that's over in a little. Anyway, we have a game on Friday I have to be back for."

"A game?"

"Baseball. That's what I was in Frisco for. We played there Friday afternoon."

"I'd love to be free like that," she said.

When they finished eating he took off his jumper and skivvy shirt and lay back on the cot and let the sun beat down on him. He looked up once and thought he could tell that behind her sun-glasses she was staring at the hair on his belly. She reached for her water glass. "Look — " she said, "would you like to meet my friends? I know you have to get back but I thought you might want to. It's just down the coast...." He liked the way she talked: always calm, lazy always, quiet, slow.

He paid his own bill when they checked out; he made a point of it even though it left him with only four dollars. Because any woman who took the trouble to examine a man's belly hair owed him something and he did not want to complicate that debt with money.

◆

"And this is Solly — Mr. Stahr," the blonde woman said.

Solly was a short, boyish-looking man with a shock of brown hair that stood out above his forehead, and big, wide, surprised eyes that narrowed slightly when he looked at you, and he had a long, hollow-cheeked, darkly tanned face and large white teeth and a quick, friendly smile.

"Solly is a writer, too," the woman said. "Like Richard. But Solly is not finding work right now." The woman's name was Arlene; she had a very slight German accent; she was Richard's wife.

When her husband came out of the kitchen carrying two glasses she clapped her hands, then frowned when he held the glasses out to Barry. "Barbara wants you to fetch hers, if you will," Richard said. "She's a Manhattan drinker. One an hour. A system for everything."

Very carefully Barry made his way across the thick rug, hoping for Christ's sake he wouldn't spill the drinks. As he turned into the hall he heard Richard laugh behind him and say, "Solly, I guess you're not one of the chosen people tonight...."

Barbara was sitting at the edge of the bed, talking into a white phone. She had changed into a white blouse with heavy copper buttons, short black skirt; the belt wide and shiny black, with a heavy copper buckle.

There was a row of windows on the room's three outside walls and half her face was in light, half in shadow. "Yes, yes," she was saying, "I will." She looked up and beckoned with her free hand and he went cautiously across to the bed and gave her her drink. Then he stood looking out a window across the back lawn: not far distant — maybe it was a quarter mile — he could see the ocean and he wondered how long ago it was that Richard had made his first million. Richard was tall, maybe six-six, and thin, and pale with a long nose, and not Barry's picture of a millionaire — and his wife, short and almost stocky, blonde and pink-cheeked, not a millionaire's wife, or even Richard's, for that matter. But opposites attract, he thought; and so does money. Or maybe it was *her* money.

"Barry — ?" She parted her lips and raised her glass to him, and so he raised his and they nodded seriously at each other and drank. She stared a moment more without smiling and then she put the speaker back to her mouth. she listened a moment and then she said, "Oh, shits," the word from her surprising him. "No," she said, "Look, I thought I told you that.... All right. I will. Very very careful.... Sure.... Yes, bye bye."

She put the phone on the floor beside the bed and took another sip of her drink and laughed softly, just once. "He's such a mother hen," she said. She stood up and went to her bags in the corner of the room. "Do you like Richard's house?"

"It's where you go when you die, right?"

"Something like that. Did you see his recording equipment and his cameras?"

"Arlene priced them all for me." He thought her face was slightly flushed.

"I always dread talking to my father. Let's just sit one minute before we go out. Is Sol here yet?"

"He is now."

She smiled at him. "Look — sit down. Why are you pacing?"

He went to the bed and sat beside her. The bourbon was beginning to warm his stomach and he was aware of her perfume.

"This is Cindy's room," she said. "You have Jon's. They're at camp, or did Arlene tell you that?"

He cleared his throat. "I was thinking maybe I'd head out," he said. "Three's a crowd and I count that many not including Richard and his wife."

"That's ridiculous," she said. She swallowed the last of her drink. "Did Arlene tell you that Richard makes eight thousand a week? Or some such insane figure. He doesn't, but that's why Sol came out."

He looked back at her, thinking that his own father had never made that much in a year, his grandfather in five years.

She touched his arm lightly with her fingertips. "Don't look that way," she said. "I'm glad you decided to come with me. Let's enjoy the evening."

◆

He sat cross-legged next to the fireplace screen and sipped his drink and half-listened to their talk. Kafka was boring, Chekhov, never; politics in California had hit a new low; so-and-so has Toulouse Lautrec posters in his dining room, if you can imagine; everything all right now, he thought, and soon to commence because before long Stahr would certainly have to leave and then Richard would wind the clock and put out the cat, so to say, and take Arlene off to bed with him, and then he and Barbara would be alone.

Earlier, Arlene had asked him, "What is your marriage situation, dear?" speaking in a whisper, her head close to his.

"Single," he answered, chewing on an ice cube, considering Arlene's pink cheeks and blonde hair six inches from his face.

"You are right. Single is best. Do you have a girlfriend, a handsome boy like you?" and he shook his head and she said, "But one in each port, I bet you," and was asking him what he did in the Navy.

"Ship's company in Dago. I play baseball. Box a little."

"Baseball? Prize fighting?"

"Anything to keep from working."

Stahr pushed the hair back from his forehead and smiled his friendly boyish smile. "Red sky at night," he said.

"That's right," Barry said, "sailor's delight...."

"Red sky at dawning," Richard finished, "sailor take warning," and then Richard began to tell Barbara about the most significant aspect of any kind of enforced confinement, such as the Navy or the Army or a prison term or a long illness, or even marriage; that the prisoners projected everything into the future — to a time when they would be free — that they existed in a dream world of release but had to live in their real world of confinement, and Barry stopped listening and poured himself a full glass of straight bourbon over the ice cubes he had left.

He refused Arlene's offer to beat him at badminton, but Stahr agreed to play her and then, after they watched a few minutes, he and Richard and Barbara went into the basement, to Richard's billiards room, and Richard explained the game to him and while Barry practiced Richard stood beside Barbara's chair and kibitzed him and then Richard played him three games, beating him each time, only the last game even close.

♦

When they went back outside, dark was settling in, and now soft, colored lights glowed from the black poles spaced around the patio.

He went to sit on the lawn by Barbara, finding it harder and harder, the more he drank, to keep at a distance. He remembered back in the billiards room, first her hand around Richard's cue, holding it for him, then her fingers around the neck of the fifth when he handed that to her, resting it in her lap, and her eyes — the whole time as he practiced — and her lips, barely parted, watching him.

Now Stahr was chasing Arlene across the lawn, trying not to catch her so much as to trip her, and he was sitting in front of Barbara and she was lying back on her elbows against a slight rise in the lawn, her legs loose in front of her, toward him, the white skin of her inner thighs just visible under her short black skirt, watching his face while he explained what it was about baseball — you had to force yourself to keep your eyes on her face; drink in one hand and watching him, her lids heavy on her eyes, a half-smile — listening to him explain what it was that made baseball so much better than boxing — one helluva lot better sport than boxing because — what was it? — oh, yes, because you could loaf at least half the time. That was it.

"That's it?" drawing her head slowly back.

"Yup, that's it."

"That's terrible." She brought her head forward again, smiled. "You'll never be a Horatio Alger hero with that kind of attitude," and then they heard Arlene shriek and looked out to the lawn past the lights and saw Stahr carrying her toward them, piggyback, trying to run with her on his back, and then Richard blinked the patio lights off and on, off and on, calling them in for dinner.

♦

There was red wine with the meal and white wine with the dessert and Barry listened and ate, eating as much as he could so that he would begin to get sober. They talked about pot and sticks of dynamite and contact highs and some woman who was the speed queen of Sausalito, almost a holy woman she was so dedicated, and nose candy, and he was mildly interested in all of it, but they seemed more serious about it than they needed to be, and they talked about in-groups and out-groups and people with names like Stekel and Rank and Ericson, and about the rise of nationalism and about fascism and Nazi Germany — "…they stopped my uncle on the street, to question him. And one of the troopers had his gun out but the safety was worn on it, they said later. So my uncle was shot six times by accident."

There was silence when Stahr finished until Richard, lighting a cigar, said, "Motherfucking soulless subhuman krauts," and Arlene said, "Whenever the children are away he gets foul-mouthed," and put her finger to her temple and continued, "but, yes, I will tell you, there were bad Germans."

"Beautiful," her husband said, getting up. "Beautiful."

And now he was sitting crosslegged by the empty fireplace, listening to them, thinking of Barbara talking on the white phone in the bedroom: maybe excited because he was in there with her, had the bedroom next to hers for that night. Maybe that hadn't been her father on the white phone: would a girl say *shits* to her father? Maybe, maybe they did that in New York, the East — or maybe it had been a boyfriend back there. Who could say? Maybe a husband.

He got up and went to the kitchen for ice. Richard was there breaking a tray of cubes into a bowl.

"I wouldn't have had Sol come," Richard said, "but Barbara didn't tell me — you...." He waved the empty tray.

"It's okay. I went up to that fellow's place with her, you know, Hobson's."

Richard drew on the stub of his cigar and then dropped it into the sink. "Yes?" His eyes narrowed above his long nose.

"Do you know him very well?"

"I know him." Richard put a long, bony arm lightly across his shoulders, started him toward the door. "Barbara's perfectly safe, my friend, as long as she doesn't do anything rash."

When they entered the living room, Stahr said to them, "I just gave the song which is Solomon's, my own canticle." He smiled cheerily. "I'll do it again if you like." He took a deep breath and then in an earnest, slightly quavering voice he recited:

> "Western wind, when wilt thou blow,
> The small rain down can rain?
> Christ, if my love were in my arms
> And I in my bed again!"

He looked at them, looked at Barbara and Arlene on the far couch. "What kind of poetry do you like, Barry?" he asked, smiling.

"I don't know any."

"Oh, but you knew 'Red sky at night.'"

"You have to know that if you're in the Navy." He was beginning to dislike Stahr.

"Beautiful," Richard said. "Beautiful, beautiful. *Très classique!*"

"He is joking, Solly," Arlene said. She leaned forward. You know, everybody, Barbara and I have a secret — "

But Richard interrupted. "Jesus Christ, Arlene, don't be so fucking stupid." He turned, looked across the room at Stahr. "And the poets aren't the uncrowned legislators, Solly. They're just uncrowned. That's one of your problems."

"Leave poor Solly be," Arlene said.

"Sol," Richard said. "You've got a problem."

"I *have*. I have." Stahr clasped his hands between his knees.

"No," Richard said, "I mean you should be what nature meant you to be. Quit fighting it."

"Which is? What's that?"

"Another Oscar Wilde," Richard said and began to laugh, choking on his cigar smoke.

'The damnable thing about it, Richard, I keep thinking I *should* seek out — "

" — that certain someone," Richard finished. "No soul-baring now, Solly. You've had your chances, right? You've rolled the dice."

"Yes. Oh, yes. The thing is, I know I *ought* to be able to love someone enough to marry them, yes I have loved someone enough for that, God help me, I have, but...."

"But what it comes down to," Barbara said lazily when Stahr's voice trailed off, "is that it's probably just too much trouble. Too messy. Too many ties and obligations. Was that it?"

"No. God help me it wasn't that, Barbara. When it came down to it — I don't know. My psychiatrist doesn't know either." He brushed his hair back, tried to smile at them. "You see, according to him, I'm too involved with myself, too bound up in my own problems to have the range of sympathy... the range of sympathy that...."

"You mean," Barbara said, speaking very slowly, "that you don't seem to have the range of sympathy needed to enter into the individuality of another person, someone else distinct from yourself, is that it? Or more than one other person. That you can't realize an *Other*?" Stahr was nodding as she spoke. "That you feel the obligations but can't *realize* them because...."

"Oh, horseshit," Richard said calmly.

Arlene rose from the couch and went to Stahr. "Come, Solly," she said. "I'll fix you a drink, poor dear."

"What are you drinking?" Barry asked. "I'll get them."

"Not for me," Stahr said. "I think I probably have had too much already."

Stahr turned away from them and went to Barbara on the couch and spoke to her in a low voice and then turned and crossed the room back to them. "Goodnight, Richard," he said. "Arlene. Thanks for having me." He looked at Barry. "Come out with me?"

Outside they walked silently to the drive and then before getting in his car, Stahr turned to Barry and held out his hand. "I like you," he said. "You're all right. You'll be good for her."

"Yuh," Barry said. "Good to meet you, too," thinking — you poor simple bastard. He turned and went back across the lawn to the house. Above him, the sky was a blue-tinted black, sparkles of cold white spread across it.

◆

"Will you get me, then, a double, please, dear?"

"What's your husband drinking?"

"Richard is in bed. Richard does not like Monday night parties."

He got them drinks and sat down on the floor with his back against the couch that was at right angles to theirs, one lamp on a low, square glass table between the two couches lighting the room.

"How can you go on drinking?" Barbara asked him. She turned to Arlene. "It's two-twenty."

"Just one," Arlene said. She put her arm across Barbara's shoulder. "I am a tolerant person — Barry, dear, you should pull closer here. I will tell you some things a good boy like you would not believe, even a sailor." She smiled, winked at Barbara. "Because of such wickedness that goes on here."

"Oh, yes," Barbara said. "Sodom-and-Gomorrah-land."

"A person's own *husband*," Arlene said. "But he will do anything to get money, that Richard. People say I am materialistic, but when my babies were born I knew who I was, oh yes. You should have such an experience." She laughed. "But of course, Barry, for Richard it is either money or sex, I tell you — "

She talked for the next half hour, and then asked Barry to get her a fresh drink and then she talked for another half hour,

15

endlessly on. And Barbara watching him as Arlene talked… All she has to do is leave, he thought, go to her bedroom. Some signal.

Once he managed to interrupt long enough for "There's a lot to be said for silence, you know, Arlene," and her eyes flashed back at him but she continued and the next time he came back from the kitchen he found himself sitting only a foot from her, close to the white knees under the short skirt, her pink calves, the gold shoes.

The next time he left for the kitchen he heard her say in a loud whisper, "Why are you staying up, Barbara? Can't you see he is not sober?" and suddenly he was angry. He put the glasses in the sink this time and when he entered the room he said, "Arlene, go to bed now." Her eyes widened. "If you don't, I'm going to get your husband up and he'll drag you to bed by the hair."

"Well," she said, rising unsteadily from the couch.

"It's almost four o'clock. It's too late for this anymore. You're boring us."

"*Well*! — That is one thing I am *not*," she said emphatically. "I am *not* boring. I have had offers, you know. Plenty of." She started across the carpet. "We have been in the movies, haven't we, Barbara?"

♦

He went to the light between the couch and turned it off. Then he stood before Barbara and looked out at the sky through the window behind her.

"Is the sun coming yet?" she asked.

"Almost. That Arlene — she wouldn't stop talking. Why?" He sat down next to her and put his arm across her shoulders and she leaned against him, her head on his chest, and he lowered his face to her hair. Her hair had a pleasant fruity smell — but everything seemed distant and unreal, even her hair against his cheek.

"All kinds of rivalries tonight," she said. "I'm so tired. All kinds of private worlds, everybody off in their own."

When he turned her head and kissed her, she opened her mouth and he waited, holding his mouth against hers and stroking her dress, first her blouse and then her skirt, and when she put her tongue in his mouth he let his hand go under her skirt and reached up between her legs and began to stroke the smooth fabric there, and finally she moved her legs, opening them slightly. He kissed her and touched her, stroking her, and then he took his hand from beneath her skirt and unbuttoned two of the copper buttons and reached into her blouse and began to stroke the soft upper surface of one breast. He reached into her bra with his thumb and forefinger and took the nipple gently and then he released it, still soft.

He stood up and took her by both hands and raised her slowly to her feet. Her head came to the top of his chest and she was looking into his eyes, her own only half-open, her lips just parted. He could not see the color of her eyes and for one moment he had a great feeling of sorrow for her and did not understand why.

He bent and lifted her and turned and walked off with her toward the hall, stumbling a little and thinking that this was foolish and that maybe he *wasn't* sober.

In the bedroom he put her down carefully on the bed and shut the door and turned the knob-catch and then went to the bed and lay down beside her and began to kiss her. In a few minutes he stopped and drew his head back to look at her; her half-lidded eyes were looking back at him and he could not tell from them what she wanted.

There was a single light tap at the door and a voice said, "Everything is all right, Barbara?"

"Yes," she said, smiling at him when she answered. "Thank you, Arlene."

He kissed her throat, mouthing it, and unbuttoned the rest of the buttons of her blouse and then he reached down and drew the bottom of her skirt up to her stomach. He kissed her mouth and put his hand beneath the top elastic of her panties and felt the stiffer, bunched hair there and he began to stroke her with his fingertips. She put her hands at the back of his neck and kissed him and after a few minutes she began to arch against his hand.

They drew their heads apart and she said. "The only trouble is, I didn't come prepared."

He waited, neither of them speaking until finally he said, "I haven't anything with me…. You have sad eyes."

"All Jews have sad eyes," she said softly.

"Are you Jewish?"

"Does that shock you? I'm half-Jewish. So I'm only half-sad."

"Sure," he said, smiling. "But it's still six of one and a half a dozen of the other to a Lutheran. Here — " He took the top elastic of her panties and began drawing them down over her hips; she arched her back, lifting herself away from the bed, raising first one leg and then the other as he pulled her panties over her feet. Her hair was black, as black as the hair on her head and thicker than that on her head, and it extended upward almost to her navel, a heavy triangle with its upper border extending across her lower belly. "Here — " he said again and put his hand on her bra over one breast and lowered his head to her stomach and put the tip of his tongue in her belly button and then down to her hair, feeling it stiff and yet soft, and breathed into it, liking the pungent scent that came to him from it, wondering why he was doing something he'd never done. She put one hand at his head and stroked his hair once and he started downward, tonguing her hair slowly until it was wet and until he came to the cleft where her flesh was closer to the surface beneath the hair and where it was already moist and then he began to tongue the lips of her cleft itself, and he heard her sigh above him, a long, weary sigh.

He lifted his head and scraped the flesh of her inner thigh lightly with his teeth and she sighed again. He took her hand from his head and put it on his blues. In another moment he placed her hand on himself inside his clothes.

She opened her legs when her hand touched him and so he put his tongue into her and moved his head, liking and disliking the sour taste of her, but liking the feel of her on his tongue, first soft and moist and then stiff hair and moist again. He raised his head from her and straightened to a sitting position on the bed and turned himself, drawing his trousers and skivvies down to his shoes as he turned and then he put his head between her thighs again, opening the cool whiteness of her legs with a thrust of his head, and he felt her take him in her hand again and then he felt her lips over the head of his cock and then below the head, and suddenly, for a long instant, he was so content and at rest that he knew that this must be what people went to hell for because anything so full of pleasure had to be forbidden, and he turned his head on her, the cool skin of her thighs against his ears and cheeks, and he took the swelled lips into his mouth and drew on them, gently at first and then harder and then he thrust his tongue into her, scraping his teeth gently across her lips until he began to hear her breath rasping through her nose above him, and he could feel her mouth growing frantic on him, over and back, over and back. Her hand had released him when she took him into her mouth, but now she grasped him with it again and began moving him into and out of her mouth, more rapidly each time.

She began to arch and squirm under his mouth, her legs full apart now, and the smell and taste of her were strong and pleasant to him and he continued — continue forever, he thought, but lying there, wanting it to continue, he began to want something more final, and his tongue was beginning to tire, and he did not know what the etiquette was: this was not Tijuana and she was not a whore and he did not know. He raised his head to her stomach and began to tongue her belly button, the dry skin of her belly warm against his cheeks, and then she took him from her mouth. "I just remembered," she said, "I do have something."

He rolled away from her and put his feet on the carpet. He bent and took off his shoes and socks and stepped away from his trousers and skivvies. "You do?" he said, standing and loosening his neckerchief and then peeling his jumper and skivvy top over his head, thinking he should have been smarter, should have known that this was only supposed to have been another bellboy's errand.

"In my green bag. On the dresser."

He walked to the dresser, the room almost fully light now, and in the green bag under the flask he found a blue paper sack, *Rexall* in small circles patterned over it.

"Solly was in the Marines," she said.

He took the small flat box out of the sack. There were three condoms in the box and he opened one and put it on himself — not unrolling it all the way because he had grown slack thinking about the bitch trick she had been playing on him and yet she had waited all night and into the morning for this; he was too weary to begin to understand why.

"But then he changed," she said. "Everybody changed. It was like nobody believed in God anymore, do you know what I mean? There was no *order* to anything."

It was the first time he'd heard her speak as if she were not calm, not cool.

Before he turned back to her he looked out of the window at the white sky, listened to the birds just beginning, shook his head once. He had a strange feeling because here he was, finally, in the kind of situation he thought about most of the time with any woman — a sailor's dream, nothing less — and now it was real and there were so damn many ins and outs to it that just at this moment it hardly seemed worth it.

She was propped on her elbows under the spread now, shoulders and head on a pillow against the headboard, looking at him, her hair falling down and spreading against the white pillow-slip.

"When you were standing by the window," she said. "I haven't seen that look on your face before. With the light on the side of your face. I think that must have been what you looked like when you were a small boy. As if someone had deserted you."

He took the edge of the spread from her hands and pulled it down from her and studied her body and shook his head, his lips set without a smile. If there was anything in the world more beautiful than a woman's body, he thought, a woman's body against a white sheet waiting for you, he could not even guess what it was, her breasts flattening against herself but still full, the nipples like dark red berries, still soft, like fruit gone overripe, her belly button, her black hair, her heavy white hips, thighs. Nothing in God's world. Even her toes, pink at the tips, the small, white, blue-veined feet.

He lay down beside her and put his left hand under her head and kissed her mouth and then her breasts, squeezing the nipples gently between his teeth, and then he raised his head to look into her eyes because he had the queer sensation that she was growing younger as she lay there. Her eyes were wide open and she put her hands on his shoulders and drew him over herself and then she put him into herself. He waited, kissing her, watching the dark lids lower part-way over her eyes, listening to her breathe and then feeling her begin to move slowly under him.

He thrust up into her and returned and she put her arms around him, locking her hands behind his back, and he reached down and put one hand under her buttock and slid it up the curve of her leg to bring her leg over his hip, and she raised her other leg and crossed her feet over him, arching herself to his slow thrusts and then he turned across her and put his right hand on her hip to hold her in purchase, both of them slowly moving against each other. He felt himself grow large in her and wished she would open her eyes — because he knew he could read her thoughts now if she would only open her eyes.

He scraped her nipple against his teeth and let it slip from between closed lips, and raised his head from her breast to put his mouth on hers and then in a little more time he asked, "Can you come?" and she said, "Yes," and so he stroked then in earnest, her hips thrusting back at him, and she brought one hand quickly down behind him and pulled him against herself even harder, and then she locked hands across his back again, pounding against him, and finally she began to shudder, pulling him to herself each time and he said, "Are you?" and her eyes opened but he saw only white and so he let himself go and forgot her and finished... like turning a key in a lock, the tumblers clutching at the key.

When he had taken most of his weight from her, his palms now on either side of her shoulders, arms locked straight at the elbows, he began very slowly to move back and forth within her, letting the head of his cock come nearly out each time before moving it in again, and each time the movement brought a sound from her. When at last he was altogether soft she lay there then, quiet, and he looked down into her eyes. Her eyes were brightly soft and wide open and looking back at him, the outer ring of each pupil brown and darkly flecked; eyes like those of a 12-year-old girl, he thought, innocent and trusting, and her face was relaxed and seemed peaceful — seemed both happy and melancholy, both at the same time.

"That was dumb of me," she said. "To forget I had something."

The hair on her forehead was damp and he bent and kissed her mouth lightly, thinking that if she wanted him to believe she had really forgotten, he would.

For a long time they lay like that and then she said, "Okay," and tapped his chest once with the heel of her hand and he eased backward and started to ease himself out of her. "Careful," she said and he felt himself free and looked down.

He looked at her. "I lost it," he said, thinking Christ, what a *stupid* thing to do. "Inside you."

"Damn." She put her left hand palm up on the sheet beside her head. "Here."

He eased himself down beside her, his body touching hers, and she touched her head to him. "My father warned me against hitchhikers," she said softly.

"He was right."

"Are you a good baseball player?"

"I'm a better boxer."

"What does it matter, huh? Just so long as it's only something a man can do."

"I guess so. But you go out and play or you box someone — you do the best you can, you feel pretty good after. That's all I know."

"Do you feel good now?"

"Barbara, I don't know if you're supposed to say thanks, but — "

"You're not."

He grinned. "Better than giving money.

She did not smile and he said, "Not funny, huh?"

"Hilarious."

With his thumb he began to stroke the damp hair at her temple.

"That's nice," she said. "So nice. Is it worth it to you now? Getting back late?"

"You're different like this," he said. His thumb traced her black hair against her temple.

"You're sweet," she said.

"Yuh." His thumb slowly stroked her hair against the thin bone of her forehead. "What about the other? Shouldn't you do something?"

"I guess that's my problem, isn't it?"

"Not just yours. Wouldn't Arlene have a douche?"

"It's in the bathroom — which is through their bedroom, so… it's not your responsibility, anyway."

Her words angered him, and made him feel stupid again for losing it. "I could go in and ask her for it."

"Yes. Or we could just let nature take its course." She was staring into his eyes. "It all depends on how far you want to be involved… if you care about that."

It took him several seconds to understand what she meant. Her head was only inches from his own and he could see deep into her eyes. He lifted his thumb from her hair and formed the words of betrayal in his mind, not finding a way to soften them, wishing she had not laid herself open to him like this. "I'll go ask her for it," he said grimly. He got off the bed and began dressing.

"But if you don't want to get involved with them — then why are you…."

"With *them*?"

"Yes. If it embarrasses you, don't. What did you think I meant?"

"I thought — I don't know."

He shook Arlene and told her what he wanted. At first she did not understand him and then, when she did, she did not believe he was serious, but finally she got out of the bed and brought him a long flat box from the bathroom. "You are joking," she said, falling back to the bed again.

◆

He was resting on top of the spread when Barbara returned. At the end of the bed his foot moved every ten seconds.

"Relax," Barbara said. She was wearing her loose dressing gown. "I found it." She came to the bed and lay beside him. "It's okay, I think. I'll write you in a month. Don't worry. You have no ties. Besides, I'd know if I was. The only time I was pregnant I knew it that instant."

He turned his head to look at her. She looked small and young beside him, her body concealed by the loose, short gown, and yet she had been places he had never been, knew things he would never know, maybe had done things he could not even imagine. And still, at this moment she seemed like a young girl lying beside him, asking him to be her friend by telling him secrets, and he decided not to ask her if it had been Stahr she had gotten pregnant by. He raised his head and leaned to her and kissed her throat.

She smiled at him. "So unless you carry a mandrake root in your wallet," she said, "I think we're safe."

"You'd better sleep," he said. "Aren't you tired?"

"Yes." Her hand reached out and stroked his hair once.

He got up from the bed and went to the dresser and came back with a glass in his hand. "Here," he said. "Orange juice to help you sleep. I put a little gin in it, too. I'll be out in the kitchen. I'm not tired."

"Oh. Well, look — call me at nine o'clock — will you? Okay? …Barry, before you go, kiss me."

When he bent to kiss her she closed her eyes and he thought at that moment that he wanted to marry her.

◆

In the kitchen he fixed a tall glass of orange juice and gin, half and half, and then he lit one of Richard's cigars and sat down at the table and stared out at the brilliant blue-green lawn behind the house.

He could not think it through — no, not thinking too clearly, he said to himself, blaming it on the gin and the cigar — and he thought then about courage and fear, because last night behind the smile she had given Hobson was fear; too dark in that lunatic's room to tell by more than the way she stood — but she had been afraid. And yet she had been on her way to see him alone.... And tonight, the possibility of being pregnant by someone you would never see again — wouldn't that frighten most women? And yet she had been willing to take all that on herself, and had taken it all on herself.

Hell, he thought — and outside the sun glinted off the grass. "Best fucking piece you'll ever have, swab jockey," he said aloud, trying to put his feelings at a distance with the words.

♦

She came into the kitchen at seven-thirty to say she could not sleep. He made her a glass of orange juice and put a very little gin in it and, because he had had three half-and-halfs himself, he put his arm around her when he gave her her glass and kissed her on the cheek. "Now you go back to bed," he said. "Everything will keep." She raised her hands to touch him and he was surprised at how thin her wrists were, how small her hands.

"Good morning, you two."

They looked toward the sound together. Arlene was at the door, her eyes puffy, her blonde hair disarranged.

"Yes," Barbara said. "Good morning. I'll shower and get dressed." The two women walked carefully wide of each other as they passed.

"Will you have breakfast, Barry?" Arlene asked. "What are your plans?" She went to the cupboard and took down a container of coffee.

"I was going to see what — "

"We cannot ask you to stay again. We have other guests coming. Overnight guests."

"Oh — ? Barbara didn't say.... But then — but then do you think your husband would drive me to the highway? When he gets up?"

"I think so. I don't think he will mind doing that. He will have time to do that for a friend of his own half-sister.... Wouldn't you?"

He and Richard were finishing cups of coffee — Arlene sitting between them, reading to them from the morning newspaper — when Barbara returned. She was wearing the same dress she had been wearing the night he met her — he remembered it.

"I'll back the car out," Richard said.

Barbara sat down at the table. "Are you leaving? I thought — "

"Duty calls our sailor boy," Arlene said.

He went to the bedroom he was supposed to have used and got his dufflebag and said his thanks to Arlene and walked to the front door with Barbara. "I almost forgot," he said. "Don't go back up there alone — will you. To Hobson's."

She smiled at him, drew her head back slightly as she smiled, let her eyelids fall lower over her eyes.

"And let me know about the other. What happens. Will you?"

He opened the door for her and they stepped from the dim, cold hallway to the outside and the sun struck them bright and hot, already heating the air.

"I was hoping you might... uh, be staying," she said. "At least through tomorrow. Since you're already overdue."

"I can't, Barbara." He looked out and saw Richard behind the wheel lighting a cigar. The car's horn sounded and Richard called, "Coming? You come, too, Barbara. You *all* come — *hear*?" Richard's laugh carried across the lawn to them.

"Decisions, decisions," she said and looked at him tiredly and they started slowly across the lawn, but halfway to the car she stopped. "Have a good trip," she said quietly.

Then, because he did not want to seem to pretend an ownership he did not have in front of her half-brother, a claim he had not made, and because here in the bright sun he was embarrassed that Richard was watching them, he bent his head quickly and brushed her forehead with his lips. As he drew back, he saw her eyes on his and her eyes were sad.

He looked back when he was seated beside Richard. She was almost to the house, walking slowly, her arms hanging loosely at her sides, putting one foot ahead of the other slowly, wearily, her skirt hanging limply from her hips. At the door she turned and lifted her hand to them but he did not know if she saw his answering wave.

They drove in silence until he asked Richard if he was looking forward to guests a second day.

"You mean Barbara? Why sure! Wouldn't you?" Richard smiled and then said seriously, "Sorry you can't stay on. Arlene thinks you're the greatest. The strong, silent type, she told me." He laughed.

◆

He practiced with the team Wednesday afternoon and it went all right, even though his bones ached and the muscle under his tongue hurt, but he knew what all of it was from and he was loose and easy most of practice and tired after and he took a long, long shower, everybody gone when he came out. When he opened the door to his locker his whole body shivered once, as if he had opened a cold-storage room and had been struck by a sheet of icy air. He looked up at the wall clock — six-fifteen — and thought of the sun going down and the word *blood* came to him, nothing else....

He had chow and went to the movie and at nine-fifteen he racked in, thinking he would sleep straight through because he had a lot of lost sleep to make up, but he didn't fall to sleep till past lights-out and then about midnight he woke up. After a while he got out of his bunk and went to the head and smoked a cigarette, thought about her, felt blue and mean, and very, very sad, and wished he'd said one muttering word to her to tell her he did love her and would have stayed if she'd asked. But maybe he wouldn't have. Life's a bitch and then you die. He laughed.

He went back to his bunk and got under the blanket and after a while he slept again, but then he woke a second time at four o'clock, his heart pounding, his body hot even though the barracks was chilly now. He lay there half an hour, wide awake, wondering what was keeping him awake, knowing that something was happening somewhere to keep him awake, knew it concerned her, and then he got up and put on his dungarees. He went outside and sat on the barracks steps until the mess hall opened, watched the red San Diego sun come up, and that was the way the day went — he couldn't even find sleep under the hot sun after a swim that morning and so he begged off practice and went to the Seaman's Club and had three beers.

He bought a Los Angeles paper when he left the Seaman's Club and walking to the mess hall he scanned it page by page, dreading the headline that would tell him a woman had been found strangled in a house above Los Angeles, because he knew now why he had awakened twice, why he couldn't sleep.

He decided not to eat and he turned toward the barracks. When he got to his bunk he lay down and put his arms behind his head and thought, and it was then that he realized what would actually happen, or had already happened but had not been discovered yet: she had gone to Hobson's and shot him when he led her out to his tent, left him to bleed to death behind his house — and he promised himself he would go back to Los Angeles and say that it must have been pachucos, but he knew nothing could save her.

◆

For the next two weeks he bought a Los Angeles paper every day but there was nothing in them about her or about Hobson. And then he was discharged from the Navy and he went home to Minneapolis… He hoped she would write him that she was pregnant so he could go to her and marry her, make an honest woman of her, and let her drown him in her special kind of mysterious, half-smiling, quiet, tired love and affection.

It even occurred to him once that if she wrote him she was pregnant, in the time since he had been with her it was possible that someone else — you bastard, he thought, and felt sick with his love for her; he would marry her and never ask a question.

◆

A week after he got home he called her in New York, told her he was coming to see her. "You can't, it's just… it's impractical…. Anyway, I'm all right," low, lazy voice. "Miles make a difference to your kind, not to me," he said. "Oh, that's offensive," cool, slightly irritated. "I'm sorry, Barbara. I didn't mean to be offensive," abjectly. "Look — are you — no, look why don't you hitchhike then? There are just too many people involved, too many lies.

This time I'm going to decide what's right for me, not for other people. We'll have lunch sometime, we'll talk about it, about all the things you didn't ask about my life, ever." ...Somehow he got to New York but Richard was there and they met at a New York restaurant — long, long table, white tablecloth, expensive.... "Beautiful," Richard said, "Here you are, back for more of her eenie-meenie-minie-moe. I couldn't even get Solly a job." And then Richard was gone and Barbara was there, sitting across from him, watching him, watching him with half-lidded eyes over the water glass held to her lips. He said, "I may be dumb but I'm not stupid," and she said, "Look — you're *making* me reject you," and for half an hour then he did not speak, could not, sat there staring at the tablecloth. Finally she said, "Look — there is someone. He knew how to do it before you were born. He was All-American when you were still running around shoveling snow." ...He couldn't meet her eyes and she said to their waitress, "It certainly shows, doesn't it," and then she left him and went to a table with three men and two women at it and waved to him and sat down and he awoke — he had never gotten fully asleep — and staggered to the kitchen, feeling drunk, having to put his feet down hard so they would feel the floor, shaking his hands to get the tingling sensation out of them, the dream still real and vivid. "Fuckin' dream worlds," he said.

♦

Two days after his dream he received a card with a New York postmark, no return address:

"Hi — everything fine here. Busy, busy, busy. Working
for father now. Do you miss the Sunshine state?"

With a pen she had signed the card "Barb" and below her signature, in a slightly darker ink, was written: "Vide Cant. 3:1." He understood the typed message but he did not know what she meant by "Vide Cant. 3.1."

He wished he had reached out to her with his hand when they said goodbye. He wished he had said something, done *something* to show her he loved her and did not want to leave her. Something that would have bound her to him. He wished to Christ he had gone back across the lawn and said goodbye to her decently, told her he loved her and would protect her, told her he thought she was a sweet person, very sweet, and put his arms around her waist and pulled their waists together to feel her against him there again — a way of saying it — and looked down into those sad, tired eyes and found some answer there for his own silence. He wished he had pulled her lower lip between his teeth one last time and said goodbye to her decently, instead of a nod to the forehead and off, watching her walk slowly back to the house. He wished....

He had been touched indifferently, with no malice, with even some affection, and he was changed. Perhaps he had learned something, perhaps not. Some people learn, and some people don't... Is it not so?

"Cant. 3.1" is Canticles 3.1, of course — the Song of Solomon, but not called that by Lutherans: "By night on my bed I sought him whom my soul loveth: I sought him, but I found him not."

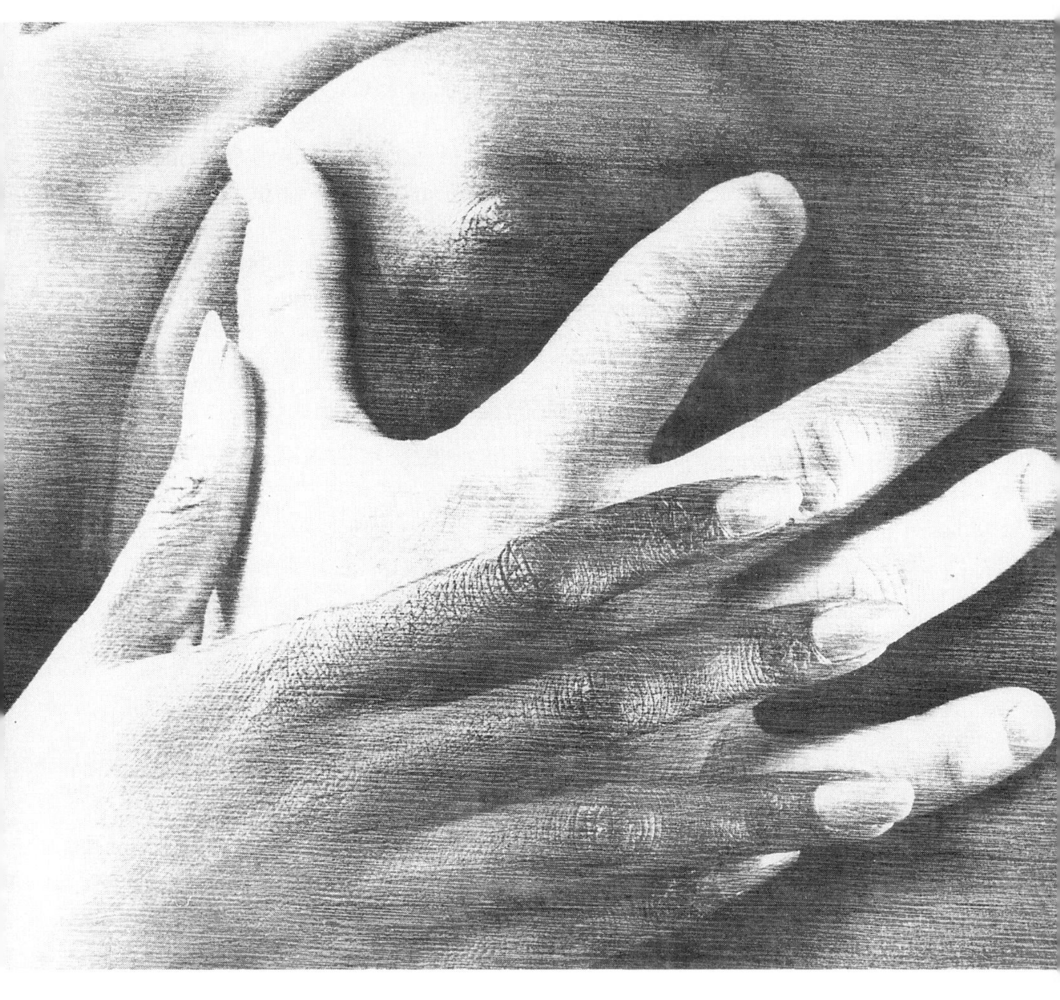

II

Helluva place for a decent, upright, God-fearing, straight-arrow Goody Two Shoes to come to search for salvation, Barry thought. He wondered if there was any booze left in this God-forsaken battleground, a bottle he'd started and forgotten, maybe.

Bartender he'd known pretty well once on Morse Avenue in Rogers Park always kept a reserve jug in his kitchen cookie jar for just such desperate situations. Guy was a big fan of British colonial movies: *Gunga Din, Four Feathers, Zulu, Bengal Lancers.* The man had studied for the priesthood, quit when he found himself getting a hard-on every time he knelt to pray.

The only thing Barry really knew about Las Vegas was that its Flamingo Hotel hadn't been named for the long-legged wading bird. He also knew he didn't like this town, from what little he'd seen of it. Ruth had picked it. Glitzy acres of slots filled with fat, pushy, pig-eyed tourists sitting on their dead duffs, buckets of coins in their laps. Ding, ding, ding — the song of the slots. Some oasis. It may not be hell, but you sure could see it from here. A good night at the machines was when it took you two hours to lose your whole stash, two hours to tap-out time.

Barry rubbed his nose where she had clouted him. If that goddam Evian bottle had been even half full, he thought, he'd have another notch in his nose. Trusting Bugsy Siegel had named his costly carpet joint the Flamingo for the color of his girlfriend's complexion — a rosy-red barn burn. Among much else, Virginia Hill liked the sauce.

"Miss Hill," the Senator had said, "what I don't understand is why these mobsters give you money. How is it you merit such expensive gifts?"

31

The crime hearings' star witness lowered her head demurely. "Senator," she answered, "I give the greatest blow jobs in the country."

And then, a year later, death had proved more of a bawd and strumpet than even Virginia Hill had for Bugsy out here in Las Vegas, where the women were usually so very friendly, so very accommodating.

Ruth had gone to have a pedicure and Lord knows what else. "It's not a luxury," she said, "Mr. Last of the big spenders. Everything's a luxury to you." He looked around their room. The Devonshire wasn't the Flamingo, no.

He could not find a stray bottle anywhere. Looking for one, he had passed his opened suitcase half a dozen times, each time feeling guilty about neglecting the work in it. 'S marvelous, wasn't it, how you could keep putting off.

Before she left, he'd asked her why she'd hit him.

"You were drunk. You were abusing me."

"Take a baseball bat the next time. Or the kitchen sink. Wouldn't hurt any worse."

"Oh, that doesn't make *any* sense. What was I supposed to do, let you hurt me? You pushed my hair around and then — "

"How come I don't remember all that?"

"Because you were *drunk*! Let me finish. Otherwise, if you don't, get out!"

"*Me?*"

"And don't come back. *I'm* paying for this room with your pushing me around, okay? *I'm* the victim."

"So what are we doing today?"

"I was talking to the maid when you were shaving. Her husband is a drinker, too. She says it's livable. She made her peace with it."

"I didn't ask about the maid," he said. "What's the schedule?"

"Oh, Terveer, you make me so *damn* mad! We'll go to lunch when I get back, what else? Give me some money, Barry, my terrible-tempered sweetheart."

Somewhat dysfunctional relationship we have here so far, he thought after she'd gone. He remembered over dinner last night promising to take her and her friend to see Ray Charles one of these nights. His guess was that her friend was an occasional Vegas hooker, but he didn't have a sure take on that. A skank, at any rate.

Given Ruth's stated reason for this meeting, he thought maybe she'd drop the games, but so far it looked like he was wrong. With him coming to her, he'd lost his leverage, apparently. Live and learn — or live some more and don't.

He remembered way back to the spring he got out of the service. There was this JC student who was getting married that June to her childhood sweetheart in their mutual hometown north of the Twin Cities. She got passed around night after night like second place in the American League. And she didn't even go through the motions of feeling awful about betraying her grade-school intended. She said to Barry once, "You decide, when you decide, who's going to fuck you. That's your business." As far as he could tell 45 years later, they all decided they would, given the necessary inducements; didn't much matter who.

True? Damn near. He'd known a second-string quarterback with the Bears once who kept track: 612 different women in four years in Chicago. Hell, he'd known women preferred cocksucking, for that matter, even though their names weren't Virginia Hill. The red-head social worker on the North Side — she had surprised him that first night, but then just about everything about sex between the sexes surprised him. Continually, and always had, from eighth grade on.

One thing he'd promised himself before he got on the plane: Ruth was not going to get him drunk and into one of those cheap chapels he'd read about out here, instamatic weddings in a wee, tacky kirk… But hell, she hadn't even mentioned it. Once again it will be proved I'm not the center of the universe, he thought — but I'll keep right on believing I am.

As far as he could tell from brief exposure to the pleasure domes, the existence of Las Vegas demonstrated that pride in hard work, civility, responsibility, self-respect — nobody cared about them anymore. Not out here under the flickering neon. Sweet little old blue-grey-haired grandma sitting next to him at the counter: "You tell your cook to get his ass in gear," she said to the waitress, "or I'll go out and tell that lazy bastard myself." Any town that hid its clocks had a lot on its conscience. A *lot*.

They cared about that stuff when he was a kid. But hell, when he was a kid, elevators had operators in them, and your family doctor came to your house if you were too sick to get to his office. When he was a kid, newsboys hawked newspapers in downtown

Minneapolis: "Hitler gives ultimatum!" "Huck Geary hits for cycle!" No more; now you got it off the TV news.

When he was a kid, his father had speed-skated at Powderhorn Park while he and his mother cheered him on. And audiences at the Orpheum didn't bark or scream their approval of an act, they applauded with their hands. And you could understand the words to songs — and women didn't regard men as their mortal enemies.

Back then, he remembered — for some reason — you settled differences after school behind the signboard, the one advertising Fords at 500 dollars. Now kids went home and got a .38. Pop, pop.

He remembered this one black 5th-grader — blacks were called Negroes back then — who got bloodied up by Cleve one recess. He was surprised what a poor fighter the kid was. Cleve was a grade ahead and a lot bigger and a playground bully, but wasn't Joe Louis the invincible heavyweight champion of the world?

Ruth owed him many, many bucks. So many he'd almost lost track. For the last 10 years, every time she put the bite on him, he'd tell her, "This is the very last you get from me. From now on, you have to make your way through life without my assistance." Huston saying that to Bogart in *Treasure of the Sierra Madre.* Him saying that to Ruth Harrison. Every time.

But he owed her one thing worth more and he tried to keep that always in mind. For a long, long while he'd practically lost the ability to feel anything. To be moved by anything. *Anything.* After the red-head. He remembered the day that started to change, which — even now, looking back on what it had cost him in dollars — he was very glad for.

About a year ago, talking to Ruth on the phone, she told him when her court hearing would be, making light of it, so when she didn't call that Friday from the Sybil Brand Institute he called out to Los Angeles on Monday. "Yes," the woman said when he finally got to someone who knew the answer, "Ruth Harrison. She's at the Chowchilla Facility. Violated. Six months."

He had sat there for several minutes after that. When he finally stood up to get a cup of coffee he was trembling and not far from tears and it had surprised the hell out of him. It had *really* surprised him — and heartened him, at the same time. He hadn't known he'd cared that much. About anything.

Those fights in grade school were something. Two scared boys in the center of a circle of very brave spectators jumping up and down and yelling for blood. He remembered them every time he boxed in a smoker in the Navy, and in matches after that.

Last night when they got back to their room she began to accuse him of various misdemeanors. He'd seen her spiral into frenzies in Chicago, but this was the first time he'd been a target.

"You were always bringing those chickies up to your place, do you remember? I do. Different little chickies every week or so. I s'pose it's still the same."

"Those were friends and acquaintances, Ruth. Platonic and political. I was working the ward for the alderman."

"I can always tell when a man's lying to me. He moves his lips."

"Ha-ha."

"Ha-*ha*? You're a womanizer, Barry Terveer. Face it. I have to, okay? You were even coming on to Helen tonight."

"To be a womanizer, means there have to be willing women. You realize that, don't you? She's your friend. I was being polite."

"Who knows what you promise them. You're no different than the rest: cheaters, beaters, and bottom feeders. Now, here, *look* at me — no, *here*!"

"Yes?"

"If it came right down to a choice, you'd let me go *whoosh* down the tubes and look out for yourself, if you had to, wouldn't you. That's how little you care about me, okay? Deep down in your heart?"

"I've got the best of intentions, Ruth, and I carry them out. I'm here, aren't I? Give it a rest."

"Intentions are bullshit. You know something I think, Barry? God is *all* that there is, the only person you can absolutely depend on, okay?"

"You know something, Ruth? God is *more* than all that there is, but even so, I wouldn't depend on him to solve my money problems. Apparently you've given me that job. Your soul maybe. Because, yes, Jesus loves you, a good Roman Catholic such as yourself."

"You've become a real prick, Barry. A prick and an alcoholic."

"Not me, Ruth. Alcoholics go to meetings."

"Terveer, you *turkey*!" she said, and her good-natured laughter made him grin along with her.

Shortly after the volleys of this exchange ended, and after she came out of an extended stay in the bathroom, a new skirmish began when he asked her what she was going to do for a job when she got back to Long Beach. That was when she clipped him with the nearly empty bottle of spring water.

He went to the chair and picked up his shirt. He needed to go out and get himself a jug. Unlikely pairing: Mr. Straight Arrow and Ms. Felonious Jailbird, at least as far as official descriptions went, he thought.

But it was like his bartender buddy told him once when they were discussing the barkeep's slightly wacko live-in woman: "Sometimes I just keep on, Barry, because I want to be able to say I finished at least one thing in my life."

◆

With the lift the second drink gave him, for some reason he remembered the time in college when he was reading a statistics text and it came to him right there, all of a sudden, that there was an infinity of universes. Not hard to imagine. God could handle that easily. For that matter, try to imagine the conceiving of a human life, he thought, how that little miracle transpired, you want to imagine the impossible.

Starting his third drink, remembering their most recent long-distance conversations, the airport terminal yesterday, he came to a decision. Based on that, all he needed to do now was to figure out how to escape from here with both of them alive.

He remembered when he first came to Chicago there was this little old lady, 83 years old, ran a bakery on the corner. She was that old and she could still bend over backward and touch her hands to the floor. She would stand behind the display case and rub her thin hands together and cackle while she told him how she'd cheated on her husband for years and years without him ever catching on. Her husband, the baker, had died when she was 38. As a young man her husband had been in the Kaiser's army. She'd stand there cackling, happy, gleeful, rubbing her hands together over something she'd put over on her Prussian task-master half a century before. Then she'd say, out of nowhere, "Without God, there is nothing." So he'd solemnly nod yes — and she'd burst out cackling again. Women remained children until they died, no matter how old, that was for sure. It is truly a long, long way to Tipperary, as his barkeep-buddy used to say.

But suppose that every time a person came to a decision that might have gone the other way, it went both ways — in two different worlds — even though you were only aware of your own one life at a time…. He hadn't thought about his college-days theory for a long time. It was the drinking did it, no doubt. And Las Vegas.

Ruth was a smooth sweet-talker when she wanted to be. She gave good phone. "I've decided there's no reason I should not have that experience," she'd said. "And you're a kind person. And smart. That's important. You're a generous person, too, Barry, and our child will be intelligent. You *know* I've always liked you, and I know you like me. Don't you?" Other times, with the bark off, she could teach those who taught classes in assertiveness how to do it. Her tongue could flay skin while she smiled.

No reason not to have a baby except she was too old at mid-40s, and if she wasn't, he certainly was. The more he thought about her proposal, however, the more flattered he was. Still, when you were young, you just did it, but not as the years went by. When you were young you could do anything. Or died trying, damn near.

An infinity of universes could account for a lot of outcomes — as they might account for a lot of dreams, say, where you were maybe crossed-over into one of the other worlds. Or maybe crazy people who weren't fastened in their own world; maybe they were hearing voices from all of them.

When you were drinking, sometimes you felt that way and things happened that didn't happen in the world you were in. He remembered one afternoon at a hunting lodge where he'd been drinking since the forenoon and about six o'clock he went to the lodge's screen door and looked up at the sky and there at the very top of a tall, very tall pine about 40 feet from the steps was a rack of whitened antlers. And the next morning when he went to the door to look at the antlers again they were gone.

Things happened in the world that couldn't be explained. They happened at random, things you had no control over, couldn't account for. Just when things got in a good groove — *whammo*! something happened or somebody popped into your life and everything changed. The only certainty was total uncertainty. You had no control. That's the way Las Vegas made him feel: jittery. One roll of the dice after another.

When Ruth left Chicago for the high-powered job in the East after the Italian dumped her she gave him all of her canned goods supply, shelf after shelf of the stuff; had him carry all of her canned goods next door into his apartment. She was extremely nervous that day and she ordered him around like he worked for her. She gave him other junk, too. A little, green box of "dip-it," told him to use it to keep his coffee cups clean. She was a stickler for cleanliness.

He remembered when he was about six or seven sitting on the front porch steps and the evening newspaper was lying on the steps beside him. The headline said that Will Rogers, the cowboy philosopher or humorist or movie actor, whatever, had died in a plane crash. With Wiley Post.

He remembered that because that morning his mother told him that Norma, the girl his own age two houses down, had died of scarlet fever. They had been close friends, buddies, playmates. His mother's words kept coming to him for about a week: that he would never see Norma again, that she was gone from this world, gone to a better one. It was a hollow, strange feeling. Put it in words today, he'd say he felt diminished. He had been a lovesick, bereaved little boy, but he didn't know it then. Sitting on the steps, watching the seeds from the tree in the middle of the front yard swirl to the ground, he glanced at the newspaper: "WILL ROGERS DIES IN PLANE CRASH!"

The red-head's name had been Norma, too. The day he met her, her roommate, who was also a social worker, had been raped in a slum hallway on Chicago's South Side. Norma had surprised him that first night. No, she'd shocked him. Because it was their first night together. She'd seemed so straight arrow until they got to his place.

Ten years from now he'd be a burned-out hulk, no doubt, if he was not there already. That was part of the reason he'd come out here. The odds were he would be needing a caretaker, and Ruth might be that person; he'd always felt good with her. Even though his heart didn't grow tipsy over her. That and one or two other reasons he conjured up after she asked him. Some of his friends who knew her slightly told him he was crazy to even consider it, but a lot of his other friends were dead in the past five years and what did they have?

You didn't need to kid yourself to believe that what you wanted in the really important things was what you actually did, no matter what it was you told yourself you wanted. That was the bottom line: what you caused to happen, what you were responsible for.

But out there in the great silence you have space-time where you could go roaming in the gloaming. And if space-time loops around — and no reason it shouldn't, since it's curved — I can enter the curve tomorrow and wind up here today, or any other time I want. Change things maybe. In some cases, yes, I'd want to. Other cases, no. But maybe you didn't get to choose.

Back in eighth grade — so he'd have been about 13 then — that winter he'd taken his skates and gone down to the park's rink as usual after supper but that night the lights were off and the warming house was closed. They'd flooded the rink and it hadn't frozen over yet, so they didn't open. He could remember what happened that night very well but he couldn't feel himself there, visualize himself that young, making that long walk, *going* there. It was as if it had never happened, not to him. But he knew it had, long ago. Like lots of other things.

Everyone else had come down, too, and if the ice had been hard they'd have been skating. Instead, kids started necking, just a few at first and then things got going and every boy was kissing some girl, and then the girls were circulating boy to boy and this went on for almost three hours. A three-hour kissing bee — unexpected and pretty wonderful, as it turned out.

It was the first time he'd kissed a girl and he must have kissed at least a dozen many times that night. It was amazing how soft their breasts were, when they had them. He'd never known that. His friend Harlan laughed at him when he told him this. There was one girl there from his class — Eloise — who was extremely friendly. She'd never looked at him before that night. Didn't look at him after that night. He chalked it up as his first lesson in the peculiarities of women. His second or third had been Barbara Mitchell and the sailor's-dream weekend he'd spent with her so long ago, so very long ago. Long ago, but he remembered her.

Were all the women who had left him in the last half century or so out there in other universes, and those he had left, and was he out there with them, as well as here? …Except there weren't so many he wanted to remember.

He almost didn't make this trip. Ruth had been acting weird on the phone for about a week and after hanging up on one screwed-up three-o'clock-in-the-morning conversation, the next day he tried to cancel but it was discounted fare, so no refund, so he came to Las Vegas. Besides, he owed the world at least one good deed, didn't he? But as he was confirming, no good deed goes unpunished.

As a boy once on the streetcar he wasn't going to get up and give his seat to an old man with a Yiddish newspaper under his arm because of the man's bloodshot eyes. His mother had taught him to give up his seat to old people and women but she'd also taught him that drinkers were bad people. His mother told him to give the man his seat; the bloodshot eyes, she said, were just old age.

Remembering this while fixing himself another drink, he was smiling in self-derision when the door swung open and Ruth shouted in a loud, happy voice, "We're home, darling!" and she strode in followed by her little friend Helen and a short, dark man he did not know.

Turned out the man's first name was Jesus — "Hay-sooz" — and he was Helen's boyfriend, or something. Scruffy fellow, torn jeans and torn shirt, but good teeth and good boots. Jesus told them a joke. Seems Elvis Presley had a brother name of Enos. So it was Elvis the Pelvis and Enos — the what? Get it? Then Jesus told more jokes: "She said to him, 'For $100 I go down on you.' 'What you do for $200?' he asked this woman. 'For $200? For $200 I do *anytheeng*!' 'You weel? Ho-kay. Here. Paint my house.'" Life of the party. Big white-toothed smile all the time.

But Helen didn't laugh much. She was sad. Her cat had crawled under the front porch of her house that morning and wouldn't come out. Not even Jesus could rescue Helen's cat and Helen was upset.

"Fix us some drinks, honey," Ruth said.

"I told you, Ruth — don't call me 'honey.'"

"Okay, then fix us some drinks, Barry-darling, *please*?"

They sat around a long time, ate the hamburgers and fries Jesus had brought, talked, Barry knocking back bourbon and ginger ale while they sipped at the first and only drink he needed to make for them. Jesus spilled ketchup all over the kitchen rug and then he rolled them joints as the afternoon wore on. Barry declined. Jesus took him aside and invited him into the bathroom to do a line of coke. Barry declined.

When Jesus and Helen left — *vaya con Dios* — Barry solemnly and formally and only somewhat drunkenly proposed marriage to Ruth, a move exactly counter to his earlier, final decision. He couldn't be sure she accepted or not, her answer was vague, but he immediately and with few preliminaries in the slanting afternoon light got laid, and that had been damn near his greatest ambition ever since he'd met her. Except it was disappointing, and he got so excited he forgot the condom.

"Need a time loop on that," he said.

"What're you talking about now?" she asked him muzzily. "Still bossing people around?" Her hair was tousled but she looked great, he thought, lying there.

She eased herself off the bed and soon he heard the shower running. Grab the money and a shower, he thought, finishing his drink, remembering that beautiful bare ass as she padded away from him.

Ruth had high cheekbones, large eyes, long lashes, a large mouth with full lips — a beautiful, almost unlined expressive face — nose maybe a little short — a young face but one with character — and most of the time, he remembered, a playful, boisterous spirit.

About seven o'clock they went out. She wanted him to take a shower before they went but he said he would later. He wanted to keep the smell of her on him. They walked for miles, hardly speaking, the evening cool and pinkly dark above. "Red sky at night, sailor's delight," he said, putting his arm around her waist and pulling her close to him. They went into Caesar's Palace, watched the table action, went up to the second floor and stopped to watch the small screen on a pedestal near the larger-than-life statue of Joe Louis. An all-white statue.

Beauty, money, power — it all came down to ownership, *control*, didn't it. I own this, look! She will do what I want, cater to me. Hell, it all came down to a beautiful woman — *yours*. You had power over her. You controlled her. She called you "dear" and "darling" because she was in love with who you were — or what you had. She does what you want because she wants to, because you're such a great guy. She was living proof you were, right? Was Las Vegas the City of Fun? Did anything go here? Would any man tell you it was power? Sure. So would any rapist.

The pedestal's small screen had about five minutes' of Louis' knockouts that it played over and over: Schmeling, Braddock, Savold, Galento, Buddy Baer, Mauriello, all of the clips showing the killing moment, with Louis moving in and chop, chop, the other man suddenly down. Joe Louis the sweet scientist, inexorable, devastating, invincible. The Brown Bomber.

"His shoulders turn into it, Ruth, see? His whole body. See it? *Either* hand. Most fighters got only one hand."

"I see it, I see it," she said, laughing. "Look, everybody," she called out. "Barry's getting off on Joe Louis!"

Later, she put $20 into the slots. He put one quarter in a machine, but only because she insisted. A contribution to Fun City's needy casino owners — who all lived back in Chicago; every little bit helps. He didn't like to gamble, but as they were leaving one low-scale place he stopped before a wheel. "Wait a sec," he said, "I'll show you how it's done." He had a feeling.

He put two twenties on a number and the man spun the wheel, smiling at Ruth. Barry was the only player. The huge wheel groaned to a stop with the pointer over the number six, his number. Ruth squealed in delight and he gave her his winnings. Figure the odds on that. He'd changed his luck that afternoon but it still held good. Unless it was a fixed-wheel come-on.

About ten o'clock they ate. He watched her push the meat she'd cut around the edges of her plate. She'd sent the steak back to the kitchen once and now she was playing with it.

"Get a doggy bag," he said. "That's a waste, not eating your food."

"I haven't seen my cat for a year, Barry. I have to get her. You could fly back with me and we could arrange things. It makes me so sad. Take your work with you."

"Why rent an apartment in Long Beach when supposedly you're coming to live with me?"

"I have to until my parole ends. You wouldn't *want* me to live in the place I'm in, Barry. But we could live here when I get off parole, okay? Jesus thinks he might be able to find me a job. But I won't live with a man unless I'm married to him, you know that."

"What kind of job would the Mexican Mafiosa have in mind for you, do you suppose? I wonder what. I like your idea of meeting me half-way, incidentally. Las Vegas: half-way between Chicago and Long Beach."

"Do you think she still misses me?" Ruth asked. "I know she does. We were so close. Poor baby, all penned up for so long."

"You or your cat?"

She frowned at him. "Of course my cat," she said. "I can't stay where I am. Two blocks away it's whore's row. I have to get my furniture out of storage. I have to get Muffy. I have to get an apartment. You have to help me, Barry. You promised."

"You won't live with someone you're not married to but you let the Italian pay your bills — what's the difference?"

"He didn't pay my bills. He never even offered. I need a car, too."

"No Sicilian backing? No Romance language dinero? Then you're lucky. Never owe money to a man whose last name ends in a vowel."

There was sadness in her face, and that small touch of coarseness to her features that made her beautiful. The trouble with me, he thought, is that I still believe the lyrics to all the love songs they played at high school dances.

"Ruth," he began, "can I say something? Will you get mad?"

"Barry, how do I know?"

"I'm just being polite. You're a beautiful woman, Ruth. How much do you rely on that stuff?"

"Stuff?"

"*C'mon*.... It makes a person awfully unpredictable, Ruth. Undependable. This one person I knew, maybe that was her personality. She was under a lot of stress most of the time. The DEA can come in and impound your house if they find any. Take your house, everything you've got."

"Oh, please."

"They can. They *do* for the hard stuff — your nose candy. It's unconstitutional, but they *do*. This addict I knew, she was only hooked on Percodan and Valium, though. Maybe redheads are unstable to begin with."

"Thank God I'm not a redhead, then." She laughed and crinkled her nose at him. "Did you listen to the Winans' cassettes? Before you sent them? BeBe and CeCe? Weren't they boss?"

"I quit listening to music after Gershwin and Glen Miller. You never liked gospel before." If you kidded yourself, he thought, his mind still on the red-head, you could believe in free will. Or, contrariwise, you could believe that everything that happens is inevitable from what went before.... But if you — a person — killed yourself, wasn't that both...? But of course it didn't make any difference by then.

"I like the Winans," Ruth said, "just because, okay? We had a jubilee gospel fest *and* a barbeque on Labor Day at Chowchilla and it was very pleasant. '*Don't you wanna go, don't you really wanna go?*'" she sang softly, leaning across the table to him. Then she said, "You always knew I do a little coke. Is that it? But you also know I'm not an addict. Addicts are stupid, do you understand?"

"Like I'm just a social drinker."

"So what are you telling me? You promised to take us to see Ray Charles, you know." She reached across the table and put both her hands over his. Her hands were in yellow rubber gloves. "We used to do coke in junior high in Chicago," she said. "We'd smoke coked cigarettes, primos. I can handle it. Here I am. I'm alive. We'll have a child and raise him and *we'll* have a home. That's all I care about. What it would be like for the two of us to have a home together. Like the two of us together here on Thanksgiving. I'm easy. You be easy. I thought you were behind that program, Barry-dear."

"Where I grew up in Minneapolis was South Side, too," he said, "but we thought coke was high-grade coal. How come the gloves, Ruth? I can understand carrying around your own water jug — in case I attack your hair again — but how come the gloves? Got a thing for washing dishes?"

"That'll be the day. Never mind. I have my eccentricities."

You could be living in your own one universe, he thought, and then suddenly you might be switched into one of the alternate worlds and you wouldn't even be aware of it. But all the bad that had happened, because of you, would have been erased. If you were switched into a *better* world, that is.

She nudged his hands. "Hey!" she said. "Where are you?"

He looked up. "You think you can lay off that stuff long enough to have a kid?" he asked. "And raise it? Give it a proper home?"

"What about your drinking? Look at you. Disgusting."

"Given the incentive, I could, sure. I haven't had a drink for — not for half a year before I came out here. This is a holiday." Little white lie, he thought. No harm, no foul.

"Well, I'm not asking for a *monk*, darling. Anyway, it's different with coke."

"Not for a fetus. No, sir. That's going too far."

"Yes, of course. I mean *you* can't know until you try. Not until you take off, okay? Everything in living color, no more black 'n' white."

"If I ever snorted coke, I'd get my nose caught in the bottle."

She laughed. She said, "No, you'd bring your guts up the first time, believe me. But be honest: Do I look like a greasy junkie to you?"

"You were using in Long Beach, weren't you. Last week. That's why you sounded so off the wall."

"Did you see that pissy little manager when we left tonight? How he looked at us? I don't like him. That is a very crumby motel, Barry. Do you realize that you're very cheap with your money?"

"I have to be. You've got it all with your hard-luck stories. I'm so broke I can't even pay attention."

"Sometimes you're funny, Barry — and then there's now. There better be more, honey-bun. I need things. Are you up for that? Money and looks aren't everything, but to me they are."

"That's a great philosophy, Ruth. If you believe that, you're out of luck. With me, anyway."

"Just kidding. Just kidding, Mr. Chintz. I told my father once he was cheap and he slapped me and told me to get out of his house. I told him, 'You're not ever going to be safe again if you ever put your hands on me again in any way.' And he wouldn't have been, either. I'd of gone for a knife. I was 16. A little coke was all that made my headaches go away. It was the only way I could live in that house." She looked at him with a sorrowful expression.

"Don't think about it," he said. "The past is past. No brain, no headaches, Ruth. C'mon, we'll go back to the room and I'll do you so fine I'll wish I was you." He noticed, when she smiled at him, that there were a few tiny broken blood vessels in the whites of her eyes.

Walking back to the Devonshire they stopped and talked to some union pickets at the Frontier, then further up the Strip for a drink, then he bought two fifths of Beam so he wouldn't be caught short again. Her moods made him uneasy. His purchase of the liquor made her uneasy, he could see, though she tried to conceal it.

Back in their room, after he made himself a drink, she asked him if they were going to watch TV or what? She had changed into shorty pajamas. She patted the place on the bed next to herself. He continued slowly pacing the room.

"You gonna work then?" she asked. "You put out that work minute we got here and you haven't looked at it. Big deal."

He went to the opened suitcase with his work in it, picked up the book from the top of the stacked papers and file folders. "Listen," he said, finding the page he wanted. He began reading aloud:

"In his appearance as in his character, indeed in his whole nature, there was something attractive, indefinable, which drew women to him and charmed them...."

"So?" she said.

"'Lady with the Pet Dog,'" he said. "Chekhov. He's describing me, right? I'd say so."

"Don't you wish."

"Well, yes, I do wish. For one thing, I wish you'd try a little tenderness once in a while. Couldn't hurt. Seems like with you it's all take, no give. I could just as well be the wallpaper."

"That wasn't tenderness this afternoon? Our little interlude?"

"Interlude? You can talk plainer than that." He felt expansive; he felt like talking. "You know about Ollie?" he said. "He was okay. Very sad thing."

She nodded vigorously. "That was *so* tragic," she said. "*So* ugly."

Ollie had been an airline flight attendant. Barry had noticed over the years that Ruth usually didn't keep friends for very long, but she and Ollie had been friends since Barry knew her. When Ollie had gotten so sick he had to stay in his apartment, Barry had given him work to do there. Ollie had died of AIDS two years ago.

"There was this stewardess," he said, "and these two guys kept hitting on her, one in First Class and the other way at the back end of the plane. This is a true story."

"Of course."

"So just before they land in Chicago the guy in the back calls her to him and hands her a key. 'This is my room' he says. 'You be there tonight at eight sharp.' 'Okay,' she says and goes to First Class and hands the guy there the key. 'This is my room' she says. 'Be there tonight at eight.'"

"Well, all *right*," Ruth said in a low voice, "I love it." Then she said, "Ollie was really sweet. You call him a fag, but he was my closest friend."

"I never called him a fag. Even though he was. He was a good enough man."

"Barry Terveer says it's all right to be *gay*? Oh, please, dear God, help us!"

"Thank you. With those few kind words you've made a happy man very old."

"What?"

"Ruth? Why do you want to have a baby now? Why didn't you get married a long time ago and have your babies then? We're pretty damn old to think about having children."

"Because I wanted a career then. Remember when I first met you? Me and Ollie down on our knees in front of my locked door and the key inside?"

"The little cupcake with me thought you were trying to break in."

"We were. It wasn't only a career. I wasn't going to let a man, any man, tell me everything to do, like he owned me, like my father thought he did my mother — and me."

"Well, I'm not your father, Ruth, even if — "

"My father? Oh, no! My daddy was a worthless excuse for a man. He did things to my mother and me I wouldn't do — I wouldn't do to *you*!" She laughed, then her face grew serious again. "Something went out of me from that. For a long time I never had the same fun as I did before."

"Before what?"

"When I was an itty-bitty baby, honey-bun. When I got out of his house I swore no one was ever going to claim *me*. Nobody. Not any man, not any woman. *Nobody*." Her voice had risen. "Not you. Not anybody. *Never*, okay?"

"Sure. But then what about the Italian Galahad? He owned you."

"That was different. I loved him, Barry. I wish he'd loved me half as much." She paused, then went on. "Or maybe I don't."

"Whatever," he said. She seemed deeply stirred.

"You know my mother put me through school. My father was long gone. Just took off on us — after he sold the house. And took the money with. I don't know how she managed. She sacrificed so much for me. I'm different now, Barry. We're going to have Thanksgiving together, do you understand?"

He raised his glass. "Okay," he said, "I think I understand. Some of it, anyway. Here's to America's most warm-hearted holiday — in America's most cold-hearted city.... But I can't see anything's really changed, Ruth. Except you don't have a job and probably do more coke now than you ever did. Where do you get the money?"

She scrutinized her nails. She said, "I wear the gloves to protect my hands if I model again. It was American scientists invented

AIDS in the first place, Barry, you know that — for chemical
warfare. They tested it in Africa but it got out of control. And
what about those black men in Alabama they gave syphilis to and
then 'observed' them for 40 years with no treatment? Do you
understand what I'm saying?"

"I read about Alabama. The other sounds like full-grown al-
ligators under the sidewalks of New York."

"Oh, yeah? Liz Claiborne — I wouldn't expect *you* to know who
she is — she's a very famous, very rich clothes designer, she won't
design clothes for blacks. She makes them so small they won't fit
black women, okay?"

"Listen, if there's money to be made on it, she'd make clothes
to fit airplanes." He went to get another drink. "Speaking of
AIDS...," he said.

"Yes?"

"Well, nothing, I guess, unless you've got something you want
to say."

"I told you: They tested us at Chowchilla."

"That was two, three months ago, in the San Joaquin Valley."
He waited.

"Excuse me," she said. "I have to use the ladies' room. I resent
your innuendo."

He finished his drink and had another half-gone before she
came back into the room. He looked at her sitting on the bed, her
long legs drawn up next to herself. He'd always thought she had
legs like Cyd Charisse, the dancer, and no one ever had legs like
Cyd Charisse — except maybe Tina Turner.

Ruth was filing her nails, but she was looking steadily at him.
There was something different about her eyes. She said, "So you
just came out here to get me to jump through your hoops, is that
it? Jerk me around? Rattle my cage?"

"I came out here to see if you were on the up-and-up about
what you said, what you planned for us."

"That doesn't account for your sappy proposal this afternoon."
She leaned forward. *"Of course I'm on the up-and-up!* Are *you*? I
notice you didn't bring a ring like I asked. I told you I wanted a
ring. I told you where to get it. Why didn't you get me a ring?"

He didn't have to take a trip into the future to see where this
was going. At the very end, when they tired of their games, they
always drove you out of your mind — or tried to. And in almost

every instance he could remember it had started with him supposedly fucking them over first, in some way he hadn't even been aware of until they pointed it out to him, as they were always happy to do. The thing to keep in mind was that if you grew to depend on them, or trusted them too far, they left you in the lurch, betrayed you in some way. That much about them was predictable.... Occasionally he had wondered if this might not be a self-fulfilling prophecy.

"You loan money to a friend," he said, "you can kiss it goodbye. The friend, too. Just like they say."

"If you'd never loaned me any money, then we could be more honest."

"You think I wanted to find out you're probably a welsher?"

"So I should marry you to clear up my debts?"

"No. So if we ever did have a baby it would have a father."

"It would have a father. Babies have to have fathers. It's a law of nature."

"A name, I mean, for crissake."

"My child would have my name, Barry, if I weren't married. He'd know who he was, what blood ran in his veins, where he came from, what rightful nation he could claim."

"I thought we were all supposed to be one nation, indivisible."

"So are we," she said, smiling at him maliciously.

"So are *we*?"

Her smile broadened into a grin. "Us women. What did you think I meant? I'm giving you your chance, Barry. Why do you want to marry me? You've always got a dozen reasons for everything else."

"I thought you wanted me to." She wasn't being very smart right now, pushing him, he thought.

"What was your reason for all that rigamarole this afternoon?" she asked. "Just to get into my pants?"

"Rigamarole?" He took a deep swallow from his drink. He was getting a little fed up with this.

"Your marriage proposal." Her eyes seemed to glitter.

"Well, it's pretty simple," he started, shaking his head, knowing he should not go on but wanting to jar her out of thinking she had the upper hand. "It's just that it's so hard to get good help these days."

For a long minute she said nothing. Then she straightened up on the bed, put her feet on the floor, and spoke in a loud voice:

"Well, *you* can kiss *my* black ass, Terveer!"

There was a great deal of shouting for the next hour and then it finally subsided in mutual hostility and they retired, her to the bed, him to the floor with pillow and spread and a blanket. He was relieved she hadn't swung on him at the height of the fracas because if she had, he didn't know if he could restrain himself a second time and she'd probably slap his white ass in jail. "I feel like I'm in a homeless shelter," he said into the darkness.

"Shut up," Ruth said, "you ought to try sleeping with seven roomies in a room this size. Go to sleep."

"I did," he said, "in the Navy. Same as prison."

Some time in the early morning she got out of bed and brought her pillow and came to lie beside him on the spread under the blanket. They slept there side by side, like children.

♦

In Chicago their apartments adjoined on the 16th floor of a semi-luxury high-rise two blocks west of Lake Michigan on Montrose. The white, modern building rose 20 stories above the surrounding brown-and-red-brick slums of Uptown, these inhabited by rednecks and a few redskins.

Across the hall, midway between their doors, was that of a Catholic priest, originally from Italy, now chaplain to the large hospital opposite their building. Ruth told the priest she too was a Catholic but he would not enter her apartment and she found this amusing. She would tease him with invitations when they met in the hall.

This was in the late Seventies and once to raise her morale when she was out of work for several months, Barry told her she had it made: she was a woman and black, coffee-and-cream-colored, anyway — told her she was halfway home without opening her mouth, for wasn't it fashionable then to hire women or minority reps? And she was both, a two-fer.

He sent her to see several people he knew or consulted for, but that didn't go anywhere at the time because when she did open her mouth she spoke her mind — a quality that was one of the things he liked most about her but which unnerved prospective employers. She was apparently so confident that she was beyond judgment that she often didn't recognize the need for ordinary tact.

At least once a week she would stop at his apartment for an exchange of information or to talk, have a cigarette and coffee or a soft drink. Occasionally she would invite him over to her apartment when she had friends in, or to listen to records with her. Her most frequent visitors were two black airline stewards, one of them Ollie, and a married couple, the Bartlows, who lived in the same high rise, the only other blacks in the building (until a then unknown Oprah Winfrey took up residence).

Every few months Barry and Ruth would go out to dinner together. He took her to Chez Paul's, the Golden Ox, Biggs, Asuma, Azteca, Riccardo's, Corona's, Diana's. She dressed up for these outings, but she always dressed up to go out; she even dressed up to go to the Billygoat or Hobson's. They only went to Biggs once; their waiter and the maitre d' made it plain the two of them weren't all that welcome. "Supercilious bastards" was the phrase that always came to Barry's mind after that when he thought of Biggs.

He learned she did not believe in paying parking tickets; she had over $2,000 worth and a lawyer trying to work a deal with the city. He learned that her parents were dead but that she had an aunt living on the South Side. He learned that she had lost a good job at a Chicago television station because she told off her boss — a white, officious, and, she said, sexist son-of-a-bitch. He took her to mean the man was a racist. He learned that she modeled occasionally, sometimes hands and feet only. He learned that she had a B.A. and an M.A. in Communications from the University of Illinois. She had six ficus trees in her apartment.

Once he got to know her, Barry's estimate was that she was highly intelligent as well as street-savvy — as well as volatile and sometimes moody, almost depressive. He learned early on that she was easily provoked — often by seemingly innocuous remarks, innocuous to him, at any rate. But because they'd become friends he seldom took special forethought to shape his speech diplomatically with her. In both these respects, he realized, they were much alike.

For her part, Ruth said, after they got to know each other, that she thought he let his prick lead him around, and she tried half-heartedly to reform him, or at least educate him. He knew that she viewed him as something of a father figure; he didn't like this but had to settle for it. He thought that she felt he was

51

smarter than she was, because he was a male and older, and he found this amusing, but encouraged it.

She asked him to read her master's thesis, insisted on it. He found her thesis unremarkable, though after thinking about it he didn't tell her that. He'd never liked columns of figures and statistics and her work was based on mass media surveys. He guessed that her committee had given her a pass, just as good-looking female drivers seldom got tickets for speeding. He didn't feel such an opinion was sexist, just realistic — but he wasn't quite sure; he hadn't been schooled to make such judgments.

About once a month the Italian came by. When he did — she told Barry once dispassionately — the visits always began with a trip to what her Latin lover called the "killing grounds," her bedroom.

Once in her apartment — it was after their first and last dinner at Biggs — she told him how she and the Italian met. In a way, in a kinky way, they met Hollywood-"cute."

She was fastidious to an extreme, and lavished dollars and time on caring for her body. Sometimes she invited him over for a drink while she finished her before-a-going-out-date (with the Italian) toilette, a two-hour process. At a party one night at his place she came to him and asked if it would be all right if she borrowed an Australian who was one of his guests. "Sure," he said, "you're free, white, and 21 — two out of three, at least."

Apparently, the Italian tolerated such excursions; more probably, he didn't know about them. A week or so later Barry asked her if she'd enjoyed her night with the Australian. He almost ended his question with "down under," but fortunately didn't because she was already angry enough. "That sleazy, no-good son-of-a-bitch," she said, her voice rich with disgust, "he gave me the crabs." She flirted with Barry, clung to him, draped herself mockingly on him when they were together with other people, but it was all play for her, all show and no go. When she wanted to rile him she called him "Pops."

She liked expensive things — expensive clothes, jewelry, furnishings, furniture, art, appliances, food, drink. There was usually marijuana on her coffee table, but he didn't join her when he visited, he went directly to the Wild Turkey. Often she would do a line or two of coke before a date.

On Christmas and on her birthday she would have him over to watch her open the presents sent her by the Italian. She delighted in the gifts, exclaiming over and over as she opened each box, "What a beautiful man!" or "I love it!" At least half a dozen boxes always: expensive clothes, lingerie, jewelry, playful gadgets — trophies that proved to her the man's devotion.

Since the Italian did not come by or take her out that often, some weekends she remained alone in her apartment from Friday night to Monday morning. When she was unemployed her isolation could last a week or more. He knew she was there because he could hear her stereo pounding away. She played the music so loud he thought he could see their common wall pulse with the beat. When it got too loud he would bang on the wall. Sometimes when he did she would call him on the phone. "Barry?" she would begin in a high, sweet, little girl voice, "Barry?" and then, in her normal voice, tell him to go fuck himself.

She met the Italian when she was newly graduated from Illinois. Her modeling agency sent six of its girls to dress up a party given in a borrowed penthouse by three mobster owners of a Rush Street night club. She was deep in reefer as she told him about it — and had had perhaps too much wine at dinner and gotten a little loud — sitting on her long, low couch, her legs drawn up beside her, one hand moving slowly and lightly up and down the back of his neck.

"…And I was a young little innocent. I didn't drink, just wine, but they gave me mixed drinks and I went all weak in the knees and one of the men giving the party came over and I acted silly with him and then I stumbled and he kept me from falling and he picked me up and put me over his shoulder and walked around with me saying, 'Have you met my new girl?' and he stopped by the piano where a lot of people were singing and he put one hand under my dress and up into me — *into me* — and took his hand out and held out his fingers and he said very loudly, 'Smell my new girl!' and I just freaked, I just *freaked*! and I guess nobody knew what to do with me I was so wild, because that's when Joe came over and rescued me and got me out of there and into a cab and took me to a hotel suite he kept for his business and that's how I met him."

He asked her the obvious question: Was Giuseppe connected? Oh, no — never. Joe owned an import firm, strictly legit; he was a solid family man with a wife and two children. "He was kind to me," she said. "He *is* kind to me."

She got a part-week job at a radio station in Milwaukee and would drive up there and stay three days a week but she wasn't hacking it financially, though apparently she was having a good time, and that's when she first started borrowing from Barry, a little bit here to tide her over, a little bit there. His barkeep-buddy warned him he'd never see the money again, but he half-way knew that. As a bona fide of her intent to repay him, however, she wrote him in as the beneficiary of her union death benefits. But of course that was only worth something if she died before he did, which was unlikely.

By the time she left — hurriedly — for what she touted as a big job on the East Coast, she owed him $9,000. She left behind the city job he'd got her as a public information officer at $23,000 a year. The building manager stopped the elevators on her the day she left because she owed $102 on her rent, but finally relented under her unceasing and indignantly loud pressure and the truckers were able to take out her expensive furniture. She'd had a check written for what she owed but wouldn't give it to the manager until all her household goods were out of the building because, she said, "He was treating me like trash."

From New York City she would phone Barry, collect, to gossip. Usually she was going with some man who only needed a divorce to marry her — though she maintained marriage was not her goal. All of these men eventually "turned on her," as she phrased it.

Just as the Bartlows had. Once when Julie Bartlow's husband had to work late, Barry took Julie and Ruth to the movies. When they sat down together in the movie house — him in the middle — he told them, "See, ladies, what you have here is your classic Oreo cookie." Ruth laughed. Julie looked shocked, then laughed, too. The Bartlows, as far as he could tell, were a reasonable, level-headed couple.

She lost her job in New York when the high-powered project folded. She had an operation for a female problem (her term, no details given except where to wire flowers to her hospital and when to call to find out how she was), later sued her doctor for unnecessary surgery, and then one day shipped her furniture to storage in Los Angeles and followed it.

He didn't hear from her for two years — he forgot about her — and then got a call one evening about eleven-thirty. She needed a letter of recommendation from him to a California state agency to which she'd applied for a job. She was living in a nicely up-scale apartment complex and had something going with the manager.

Half a year later she called him needing $3,000 or she would be in "deep trouble." The apartment manager had turned on her. Barry told her to sell her furniture, pay out of that, but sent her the money.

Three months later she called again, needing several thousand. She was doing temp secretarial work, she said, but there was not much of it. He cautiously asked her why she didn't consider hustling if her situation was so desperate. It was an attempt to discover if she was already on the meat market. When he asked, "Why give it away when you can sell it?" she hung up. She called back half an hour later and renewed her plea. "Last time," he said. "From now on you make your way without my assistance."

She came to Chicago to see Ollie in the last stages of his sickness and Barry took her to lunch at a gyros place on Broadway near Belmont. She said she had fallen on hard times — temporarily — and asked if he could help her. He pointed out that she already owed him almost $15,000. He asked her how she could afford to fly to Chicago if she was broke. She said that was different; she *had* to see Ollie before he died. That impressed him. Face to face with her he could not refuse. She was his con artist and he was her mark; that was how the chemistry between them had worked out, he concluded. Everybody's somebody's fool.

The night before she returned to Los Angeles she came to see him in his apartment. "We'll always be friends, won't we, Barry?" she asked. "To the end?" Seeing Ollie in the last stages of his disease had apparently lowered her defenses.

She changed the subject before he could reply; perhaps she was embarrassed. "Remember that Saturday morning I had you over to see *Deep Throat* on my VCR?" she asked him. That morning she had lain on the bed beside him, long legs and all, still in her night clothes with a wispy negligee over, and they had watched Linda Lovelace in what he considered a very dumb movie. Of course he was considerably hung-over.

"A turn-off," he said. "Completely."

"You can't tell me you didn't get excited."

"You like to play the prick-teaser, Ruth. I think you may not even like sex. You like to preen in front of a mirror. You're not going to be young and beautiful forever."

"Oh, now, Pops, don't get all huffy on me."

"Did you call Giuseppe this trip, or is that too far in the past?"

"No. And I didn't call Julie Bartlow either, which is what you were going to ask me next. They're no friends of mine."

"You beginning to notice a pattern, Ruth? How soon before I turn on you?"

"They told me I shouldn't be taking advantage of you. *Me* take advantage of *you*? What a laugh."

"What'd Joe do? No, I forgot. He dumped *you*. What'd you do?"

Though they were alone in his apartment, she looked to her right and then to her left before she answered. "I'll tell you what he did," she said, her voice low, "since you seem to want to know so badly. He had his wife killed. Okay?"

"No. Not very."

"She was going to divorce him and she knew more about his business than he wanted and she must have threatened him. The story in the paper was that she drove off the road into a tree, but he had her killed, I know it. Do you hear what I'm saying?"

"Honest to God?"

"I left town, didn't I? Because I knew a few things, too. Okay?"

"From pillow talk on the killing grounds."

"Yes, you might infer that."

"Why didn't he marry you?"

"He would never marry *me*. Don't be foolish. But you know something? He never *talked* to me. That was worse. Why don't you ever talk to me about your thoughts, Barry? I'm a very, very private person, but I confide in you."

"I don't have any thoughts, Ruth." She slapped his cheek lightly.

She left about eleven o'clock, kissing him on the cheek at the door. She made a face toward the priest's door across the hall and gave a flounce of her hips as she went down the hall toward the elevator and then made another face over her shoulder at him. He hadn't seen her again till now in Vegas.

♦

When he came out of the bathroom she was combing her long, thick, black hair. A wig. "We have to leave," she said tersely. "The little prick's trying to major embarrass us."

"Who is?"

"That prissy little manager. I told you he was no good. We have to be out before noon." She was dressed. She'd been down to the front desk and gotten a newspaper while he was shaving. "He told me there were complaints," she said.

"We made a lot of noise, but who'd of thunk it."

"Oh, *Terveer*! Did you shower?"

"No. I will. At the next place. In Europe they only shower once a week and they get by. Mao Tse Tung *never* showered. Listen, don't make a fuss when we leave, all right? Piss on 'em. We'll leave with quiet dignity, all right? Quiet dignity, that's the watchword, agreed?"

"*Huh*!" She stood up and strode past him into the bathroom. After he fixed himself a pick-me-up he put on his clothes and sat down to read the paper. Wasn't the first time he'd been eighty-sixed, probably not the last. The only thing you could do was leave, because once they made the call they never reversed themselves.

The paper reported that astronomers had just discovered a galaxy that up until they just now spotted it they hadn't known was there. A next-door neighbor of 100 billion stars and over-looked till just this moment! ...Or maybe God had just put it there — counting one by one till He reached a billion. Then, with a thought, multiplied those billion blazing suns a hundred-fold. Could happen.

One of the main-eventers on some casino's Thanksgiving card was quoted on the sports page: "I've prayed about it, and God wants me to fight all these people and then my job will be done." A statement like that clarified matters, Barry thought; let's hope God takes care of his opponent for him, too. All the boxing I did, and not once did I have sense enough to pray about it. Couple of times I surely should have.

There was a half-page feature about a local impresario who had a golf course out in the desert, 320 acres of greenery — aerial photo of it in color surrounded by miles of bare sand — 13,000 trees in the desert, 65 million dollars worth, plus the clubhouse and cabanas and 60 employees: Shadow Creek, the guy called it. You had to have a 100-thou line of credit at the Mirage or the Golden Nugget to play golf there. Or be Michael Jordan or Larry Bird or Kevin Costner or Clint Eastwood.

Some place out in that desert the boys had taken Sammy Davis, Jr., and put out one of his eyes because Sammy was going with a blonde actress and thus, possibly, hurting her box office pull. The Jewish Hitler, Harry Cohn, kept his word once again. Sammy quit going with that white gal.

Think of the water it must take to keep this Shadow Creek green. All that money — and the guy knew how to play God with it, make the desert bloom — but he didn't have a clue when it came to naming his very own Shangri-La. There were no creeks in a desert, and damn few shadows.

Of course, Barry thought, I wouldn't be making a prime living if monied moguls had the sense God gave green apples. Big-buck CEOs asking him to come in and tell them how to run their companies — with a little persuasion from him, of course. He drank with them, jollied them along, flattered them, laughed at their jokes, commiserated with them, and wrote the kind of recommendations they wanted to read. He didn't have the heart to tell them that if they were up to their jobs, they couldn't have been persuaded to call in outsiders to tell them what should be done. His clients were half a dozen guys sharing a brain. Sons-a-bitches were usually Rush Limbaugh conservatives, too, all their opinions direct from the Ditto man. And they may all have been white Anglo-Saxon Protestants, but in their churches Jesus never gave a Sermon on the Mount. Would have lost his congregation if he had.

He went to the door to answer a knock. The maid stood there. "We'll be checking out soon," he said. He gave her five dollars. "Thanks for everything."

"Thank you," she said, but she remained standing there, looking at him. Suddenly he remembered: this must be the woman with the drinking-problem husband. "One day at a time," he said to her levelly, and closed the door.

He had two small suitcases, one with his papers in it, the work he'd brought to finish in Vegas, the other with his clothes — and two bottles. She had two large suitcases and a garment bag. He carried hers, she carried his. At the desk he paid and asked the manager where he thought they might find other accommodations.

"I believe the Superior Inn has available rooms," the manager said.

Ruth stepped up close to the counter. "I don't appreciate the way you've treated us," she said defiantly. "Because no matter what he does, he pays the bill. I've stayed at a lot of motels," she said, her voice steadily rising. "I've been all over the country, and this place is without a doubt the tackiest, most tasteless place I've been in."

The manager had lowered his gaze to the counter and was studying its surface.

"I'm talking to you, you jerk!" Ruth said loudly. "I've stayed in places they wouldn't use this place for an outhouse. He paid for the goddam room, we're entitled to use it. Do you hear what I'm saying, you jackleg cockroach?"

"Ruth," Barry said, "quiet dignity, huh?"

The manager looked up at Barry. "I called a cab for you, sir," he said. "It's out front."

"C'mon, Ruth," Barry said. "On to another lucky, fun place!"

In the cab she said to him, "Goddamit, Barry, what the fuck are you, let him stand there and throw us out and not say a word?"

"He's half my size, Ruth."

"Listen, Barry, you seem to think this was no big deal. It was a *very* big deal. That jerk was a pussy. You can't be a champ if you don't fight back. *Goddam* it! What does it take to get you mad? You let Mr. Numb Nuts piss all over us! Do you understand what I'm saying?"

"Get 'em next time around, Ruth."

"*You* can say that, but all your life everything's been handed to *you* on a platter. Not me. Not ever me. I'm a woman. I'm a *black* woman. Every day of my life they try to shaft me, twenty-four-seven. They put me in prison for a pissy $20 worth of dope!"

"What I'm saying is that you have to play 'em the way they lay, Ruth, that's all. Sometimes discretion is the better part of valor. You go along, you get along."

"Discretion, *bullshit*! You've never been up against it, so how would you know anything? You hear me? You don't know how it is!"

"Could be," he said. Jesus, he thought, she takes on the world every time somebody looks cross-wise at her.

◆

"They're having a soldier of fortune convention here next month," he said. "This is the place for it: Weird City. You want to call down for room service?"

"Why don't you quit drinking and go and eat then if you're so hungry? I like Las Vegas. I'll be back in about three hours. I have to get a handbag and some things. The handbag is my *big* purchase for our holiday, Barry. The *biggie*! Wait'll you see it! Will you be okay? Want to come with? Get lunch? But no kibitzing. You better stay here."

"You already have a handbag. I've known streetwalkers in Chicago didn't have handbags as big as the one you've got."

She gave him a look meant to chill with its scorn. "Do you think I shop at K-Mart?" she said.

The Superior Inn had its own casino, bar, restaurant, beauty salon, gift shop. The rooms were situated on two levels around courtyards that had tropical trees and fountains and stone benches. They gave you a map when you checked in so you could find your room.

"Here," she said, and handed him a box of playing cards. "You get these every time you make a transaction. I took it for you. You were wobbling."

She had helped him through the steps of withdrawing $600 on his Master Card, moving with brisk efficiency to instruct him in use of the machine in front of the pay booth, acting as if she herself was not to be the recipient of most of the money but was merely aiding a non-coping, dimwitted friend.

"You like to shop, don't you, Ruth."

"Yes, I like to shop. What's wrong with that? Maybe I define myself that way. Maybe that's how I know who I am. I buy the best."

"Wouldn't have it any other way."

"Because I'd rather have one of something of quality than 10 pieces of junk. Let's stop this. Arguing about money is in poor taste. You're so judgmental. You're a cynic. It's distasteful to me. I'll be back about three or so. And don't spend all that time drinking. If not for you, then for me. If you hurt yourself, you're hurting me."

"Ruth, do you mind the difference in our ages?"

"I prefer older men. I quite like the fact you're older. Why don't you shower?"

"Well, no, I meant *your* age, actually. I prefer them younger —
26 is my favorite age, tell the truth."

"Dream on," she said.

After she'd gone he made himself another drink. The thing is,
he said to himself, I never know whether to believe her or not.
"Love ya," she said when she left, but maybe that was the new-got
cash talking. And loving him was not the same as being in love
with him, was it. She'd signed her prison letters the same way —
"Luv ya" — and there was rarely any true feeling in the letters that
he could find. Maybe he hadn't looked hard enough. Maybe he
kicked up dust and then complained because he couldn't see.

He took the Chekhov book from the opened suitcase of his
work, riffled its pages to the last paragraph of the last story:

> "And it seemed that but a little while and the solution
> would be found and there would begin a lovely new life; and
> to both of them it was clear that the end was still very far off,
> and that their hardest and most difficult period was only
> just beginning."

He sighed. He said, "Yes," and then "Now you see it, now you
don't." He stared ahead, looking at nothing. At last he stirred and
said, "Dark but lovely." The right woman can make you, they
said, the wrong one can break you. But which was which?

He could remember damn near everything that had ever
happened to him. He could pretty well recall most of the women
he'd fucked, lain close to, held. There weren't that many. There
weren't close to 600, that was for damn sure. If he hadn't drunk
so much over the years, he probably could remember each one of
them a little bit better. Put on some speed, follow my lead.

In high school he drank — mostly beer — because it proved you
were a man. Later on, after the Navy and college, he drank —
mostly hard stuff — as a reward for a week's work. Once it became
a habit, it stayed that way, no longer confined mostly to weekends, even after he was no longer good at it. He remembered his
surprise one Monday morning to stumble out to the kitchen and
find the wastebasket jammed with empty fifths he couldn't
remember buying. But he did remember that he was the only
person at that particular party.

All happy drunks are alike, he thought, and there are very few
of them. All unhappy drunks are also alike, and our number is

legion; we are the soldiers of misfortune, with self-pity enough to go around twice. And I can whine as well as the next white boy, he thought.

His flight had arrived on time at Las Vegas. So had hers, but she wasn't on it. She arrived two flights later.

Maybe he should get some breakfast. A whore's breakfast was orange juice and coffee; a drunk's, bourbon and branch water, so he knew what profession one of them practiced, at least. The sun never shines in Whiskey City, it just rains Jack Daniels all the time. Are you married? Why? Do I look that miserable?

He sat up straighter in the chair, shook his head, considered a moment whether he should try to get in a little desk time, decided against it in his present condition.

The thing is, they danced better, jumped higher, ran faster, fought tougher, took more joy in life. Took more joy in eating, drinking, and glorifying the Lord, so to say. And they correctly clapped on the afterbeat. Whitey didn't. Or maybe he only knew the wrong kind of Whiteys. The time and truth of it was that he was a bred in the bone WASP.

They sure as hell sang every kind of song better. They even Sang "The Star Spangled Banner" better — listen to Ray Charles or Whitney Houston — but why blacks would want to brag on freedom's banner was a mystery. Black men couldn't *buy* a job in this country today, or any day, and Johnson & Johnson sure as hell weren't making skin-color band-aids for them.

Ray Charles. He'd promised Ruth he'd take her and Helen. He'd have to figure a way around that. He didn't want to leave this room now they were situated. He was determined to keep this room a peaceable kingdom — no shouting matches here — a sanctuary, more or less, in which to resolve their differences — once they figured out what they were. It was possible they could get along fine — not probable, but possible.

Drink a little today, he thought, then swear off and give it hell tomorrow. No, not tomorrow; tomorrow was Thanksgiving. Still, maybe so; one good morning's work and he'd be on schedule again. Complete the final report — 100 pages, plus documents (CEOs loved "documents," and never looked at them) — have it typed in Chicago, and give it to Federal Express. Then call the client to tell him the deadline was met — and probably be told by the client's secretary that her boss had just left for three weeks in Jamaica.

...Drunk half the time, you had to work twice as hard the rest of the time. Right, Ruth? When she finally arrived at the airport Monday she came to meet him on the lower level. Big beautiful smile, but when he approached to greet her she gave him her cheek to kiss, holding herself away from him.

She told him she'd tried to call him from the plane. He wondered why she hadn't called from Long Beach when she knew she was going to miss her flight. He guessed that she'd gotten fucked-up on dope the night before — and fucked, too, for all he knew. He wouldn't ask — no, sir. He should have cut his losses then, but he was lonely enough not to, that must have been it.

She had the cab driver stop at a convenience store on the ride into the Devonshire. She needed a supply of Evian spring water. It was then that Barry noticed the holster with the plastic bottle of water in it over her shoulder. Apparently, citizens of California had to carry their own private supply. Which probably came straight from the tap before the bottler slapped on a label. Try spelling *Evian* backwards. That should be a clue right there.

She also grilled their cab driver on the best places to shop in Las Vegas, the biggest and best malls, where the upper-scale stores were. Then she and the cab driver discussed the merits of the entertainers in town, agreeing that Ray Charles was numero uno.

She led the way into their room and the first thing she said after throwing her garment bag on the bed was, "Now, *no* pictures. I know you're dying to take nude photographs of me, but you can't. Do you hear what I'm saying?"

"I'm not deaf, Ruth," he said. He hadn't even brought a camera.

The thing was, the coldness at the airport and now this, it put him off, far off. It was then he decided, then and there, to drink this one out. She could traipse off and do all the shopping she wanted, but he was drinking this one out.

She was supposed to have fallen into the arms of her knight in shining armor, wasn't she? Wasn't that the way it was supposed to work? He may not be the man some girls think of, but even so... he carried the key, didn't he?

Fixing himself a drink in the kitchen he thought about the first and only black girl he'd ever seen in the flesh — before yesterday. To save money, he and his friend Harlan had walked eight miles to the Minnesota State Fair grounds in St. Paul, home of the sun-burnt Swedes.

First they watched some sulky races, then they walked slowly through the exhibits, stopping a long time to inspect Al Capone's armored Cadillac, then went to look over the Percherons and Clydesdales in the horse barn. Then, at dusk, walking along through a nearly deserted Midway, they heard a low, conspiratorial voice: *"Boys*, want to see how it works?"

They paid their quarters and went inside the tent. Maybe two dozen empty chairs. They took seats in the first row and after a few minutes an old, fat man limped out from behind the canvas curtain onto the small platform that served as the stage. In a few minutes more a young girl came out from behind the curtain. Her skin was a light brown and she was nude.

She stepped up onto the turntable in the center of the platform and stood there motionless, arms at her sides, large, unblinking eyes gazing out over them toward the tent's entrance.

The old, fat man began to tap on a small drum and the turntable the girl stood on began to revolve. She didn't move but the turntable made three slow revolutions. He could, to this day, see the dark areolas twice as big as half dollars surrounding each of her nipples, the fullness of her breasts, the gentle swell of her belly, her deep navel, and the thick screen of black hair below it.

After three revolutions of the turntable the young girl stepped down from it and went back behind the curtain. Now the shill was standing behind them, leaning over. He said that for 50 cents more, each, they could *"really* see how it works." They paid at once.

Barry knew back then, that fall when he was 14, that he would never in his life see anything more heart-stoppingly beautiful than the young girl slowly revolving on the turntable, her arms at her sides, immobile as a statue, black and lovely. Because it was the first time and there is only one of those, of anything.

That winter when the Lutheran minister read parts of the Song of Solomon to Barry's confirmation class, explaining that the Song of Solomon was an allegory of the story of the church, Barry went to the Terveer family Bible: "The joints of thy thighs are like jewels.... Thy navel is like a round goblet.... Thy two breasts are like two young roes that are twins... the hair of thine head like purple..." He knew exactly what was being described, black but lovely, because he had seen it. "The mandrakes give off a smell, and at our gates are all manner of pleasant fruits, new and old, which I have laid up for thee, O my beloved." His first doubts about the Lutheran church began about then, when he discovered that Solomon's bride was black — because the minister had neglected entirely to mention this.

Behind the curtain, the young girl, still naked, lay on her back, her arms over her eyes, on an Army cot. With their shins against the frame of the cot, pushed that close by the shill, they watched as the girl began to squirm and twist from side to side. Barry remembered his eyes did not leave the screen of hair at the center of her body as it parted to show the lips there moving with her writhings. When he and Harlan left the tent they could hear the old, fat man coughing violently. The thought had occurred to Barry on the eight-mile walk home that the girl had been drugged.

He was several drinks into it now, at the point where he thought he might catch a glimmer. Naw, she wasn't drugged, he thought, that was just an adolescent imagination at work. Sometimes he felt this same way when he listened to music. Going with the music he would feel he was about to understand something and his mind — or his heart — would speak to him as if saying, "Yes, all right," and he would feel suddenly at peace — lifted and at ease — as if he truly did understand. When he was drinking he would feel the same way — for a while, at least — lifted out of himself for a moment to where all was plain and simple. Solvable. Clear. Clean.

Maybe coke had a similar effect on people. He didn't want to know. It might be too good. Time in a bottle was his choice. Just enough to drink and he would feel lifted toward something, as if his mind were reaching toward something. Toward God, possibly, he'd thought more than once, but it wasn't toward God; that was too grandiose to come out of a bottle. Besides, it seemed to him that he had given up on God a long time ago, or maybe it was God who had given up on him, telling him in that way that he would never find absolution. Drinking more after that first glimmer did not get him any closer. It only ultimately rendered him unconscious.

Monday after they settled into their room at the Devonshire, Ruth retired to the bathroom. She'd been in there for what seemed like half an hour so he went to the door and rapped on it, concerned she might be sick. After half a minute she opened the door and angrily said, "Don't you know enough not to barge in on someone in the bathroom? You *never* do that, it's *very* impolite."

She was keeping him off balance with left jabs.

Remembering her ranting in the cab not an hour before, he shook his head. He'd be spending his twilight years fighting her real and imagined battles. And they wouldn't be just with whites she thought were insulting her; every black male worth his salt would resent him being with her, too, and every black female, probably. ...Pretty pickle you've got yourself into, Terveer. Quite a trap you've constructed.

Nine or ten months ago she had called him and asked him to wire her money at Western Union Will Call. She said she'd had to spend the night in a court officer's car. He told her that if she wanted, she could come to live with him until things got straightened out for her but that he was through sending money. "You already owe me too much," he said. He felt a sense of accomplishment when he hung up — and guilt, even though he knew that in the long run it wouldn't help her to continually help her. He had a difficult time with that bit of reasoning, but he managed.

He didn't hear from her again for three months. Then she called to tell him she'd been picked up for violating her parole.

From the Sybil Brand Institute for Women she explained: She had felt that her motel manager — an "Arab" — was overcharging her on her phone. She complained but when she got her third inflated bill she went down to the desk and shouted at the manager. "He was scum, Barry," she said. "Anyway, it's the kind of motel you reserve a room by the hour, a riding academy — *you* know." When she got back to the motel that night she found she had been locked out of her room. She called the police from a pay phone on the street.

The station's watch commander and another officer responded to her call and when she began to feel the commander was not taking her complaint seriously, she pointed out to him that he was there "to protect and serve," seasoning this civics lesson with a few expletives.

"What am I going to do with you?" the commander said. He told her he thought she was acting unbalanced, that if she didn't calm down she might end up committed, which further enraged her, of course, and she had to be restrained from physically attacking him by the other officer. She was taken to the station, where they turned up the felony conviction and discovered that she hadn't been reporting to her parole officer.

She claimed she had been told she did not have to. Listening to her across 2,000 miles he heard the weariness in her voice. "You go to California for a vacation," she said, "and you wind up on probation." She also told him she was suing a dentist who had put in a $500 gold filling that had fallen out — and down the drain — as she brushed her teeth.

Found guilty at a bench trial and given six months, she was sent to Chowchilla. She called him from there with jubilation in her voice. She said, "I put that judge in his place. I said to him I was a solid, middle-class American and he had no right to treat me that way!" She was calling from an outdoor phone. She yelled to someone else, "I'm talking to the man I'm going to marry!" She sounded wired.

He began to wonder if maybe she didn't actually need to have her head candled.

He sipped his drink and it came to him where his other universes theory might have originated. When you were a kid you could slip into other worlds, other times, on your own. He remembered doing it in the complete midnight dark of his room — many times after his playmate Norma died.

Ruth told him by collect calls that she loved him in "an important way," that they would get married when she was released, that he had to call the Animal Center for her to make sure that Muffy was safe, send the Center a check for Muffy's room and board, that people should love each other after they lost their looks or went blind or became crippled. There was little logic or continuity to her talk. She told him she had dreamed she was pregnant and he was walking proudly behind her, and in the next breath that he should check with her pubic defender to see if her conviction couldn't be appealed, and also with the lawyer representing her in her suit against the dentist. His phone bills were large; the private company the California state penal system used saw to that. She was a little lamb lost in the woods. The whole two prison terms she retained — and kept paying on — the Long Beach P.O. box and answering service she had gotten when she first moved West.

He mailed her a $140 Postal Money Order each month for "supplies." Twice he mailed her the quarterly 30-pound limit of cigarettes, canned delicacies and candy and nuts he shopped for at Treasure Island from a list she sent, the second box half clothes that she would need on her release, as well as shoes. She wrote with specific instructions not only as to colors and sizes but also where to shop — Jean Action, Lord & Taylor, Hunt & Peck, The Gap, Banana Republic — providing alternative selections supposing he could not find exactly what was called for. He sent her a hi-fi radio and cassette player at her request, sent her cassettes she asked for, stamps, stationery, clear-barrel pens, books.

It was while she was in Chowchilla that he made her the beneficiary of a $100,000 insurance policy on his life, one he'd taken out years before, sold him by his lady friend of that time, an agent. "This is a steal," his lady friend had said. She was able to list him as a nonsmoker because he smoked a pipe and cigars and the questionnaire only inquired about cigarettes. Ruth did not know she'd become his beneficiary and he did not intend to tell her. (The beneficiary had been a cousin he hadn't seen in 40 years who had become well-off selling sporting goods.) He figured that at the rate she was going she would certainly need money if a truck should roll over him.

When she was released from Chowchilla he said he would pay her motel rent in Long Beach until she found a job. Her only income till then, besides his help, was 450 dollars a month from Social Security-disability, that is, her cocaine problem and "suicidal depression." So he was supporting her with his taxes as well as directly. Maybe Rush Limbaugh had a point now and then.

Barry did all this because in his mind it was a contribution to charity, like tithing to the church, which he believed in but did not do. Didn't *go* to church, in fact — except once a year, on Good Friday.

Ruth's rambling, obsessive phone conversations, much less her history with authority, did not inspire confidence that she would make someone a helpful helpmate. And here in Vegas she seemed changed from the person he'd known in Chicago. For the most part that woman had been poised, commanding — very near imperious — and fun. Now she carried a huge chip on her shoulder and was more indiscreetly outspoken than ever. At times — not always — he would feel that she was simply demanding what was due her, or anyone else. And not getting it. That she struck out to avoid being struck. But you don't fight city hall. Not out in the open.

He remembered his insurance agent lady friend calling him after it was finally and forever over between them — a rupture he'd mentioned to his office partner — to tell him that his office partner had called on her at her apartment to offer his condolences and aid, if necessary. "He wanted it *so* bad, Barry," she said, "I almost took pity on him. What did you tell him about me?"

Sometimes it seemed as if all there was in the world was one dog humping another, that Genghis Kahn had had it right: The object in life was to kill your enemy, take his riches, and rape his wife. Not that he was surprised by his office partner; he'd cashed a few of those close-buddy rebound tickets himself.

Sex was nothing and it had never been anything — the act itself, that is. When you were young, it was mysterious, and that was good. But when you were young — at least when *he* was young — exerting your will on a girl, your power over her, that was what you went after.

When you got older, still the same, more or less, with the pleasure of the act a bonus. You thought that's what it was.

And all along what was good, when it was good, was the closeness you felt to someone else, as close as you'd probably ever get to another human being to hold next to you and feel secure with. Someone to love besides yourself.

Damn! And I don't even remember all their names. No woman to blame — it's my own damn fault.

He stood up and took the room key from the top of the TV set and put his wallet in a back pocket. Terveer, he said to himself, you've got to manage your life better. And pretty damn soon.

He started for the door, then turned back, took the Superior Inn's map from the desk, turned again and weaved his way to the door, key in hand.

♦

"Well, all right then," she said to him, "if you're sure, you're sure." Then she spoke into the telephone: "He says no, so it's just us. I'm going to get a facial and a massage first. Come by at seven-thirty, all right?" She listened, then said, "I'll meet you in front. Ciao..." She put the phone back in its cradle and turned to him. "So — do you like my new bag? And don't make any smart remarks."

"It's very handsome," he said. "Big *and* handsome."

"Handsome? It's gorgeous. It cost $330, so it should be. We'll have to get some more money for tonight. I got some other stuff, too."

"Lou-ee Vwee-tahn, maker of handsome handbags, *oui —très classique*. One thing, though."

"Yes?"

"The horseshoe is upside down on the clasp. Your luck will run out." He handed her two 50-dollar bills. "For you and Helen tonight. I got me another pack of playing cards out of it, so it's not a total loss, is it. But how in hell you managed to spend what you spent this afternoon I couldn't guess."

"Thank you, Barry," she said happily. "Helen says mucho grass-ass, too — *grazie a Dio* — and her cat is still under the porch, she *thinks*. She's putting out food but it's not being eaten. She told me she thought you're 'impressive.'"

"Well, aren't I? When are we going to have a talk? What good are two degrees in communications if you don't use them?"

"I signed up for a facial and a massage at four-thirty."

"You got time for a little interlude?"

"Interlude?"

"It's your term. A little slap and tickle. A little down and dirty. A roll in the hay. In short, my ashes hauled. The wild thing."

"Ho!" she said, and laughed. "You haven't taken a shower."

"How about we take one together, my irreplaceable you?"

"You've had too much to drink, Barry. I don't bed drunks."

"No. I'd eat you out till your skull caves in on your belly button, Ruth, I'll get you pregnant with saliva. That way the baby'll be my spittin' image." He grinned at her.

"Don't be crude, Barry. I've got to go. I have an appointment. I should be back by six. You want to eat then?"

"I'm saving space for tomorrow's turkey."

"That's *right*! I've lost track."

"But bring me an egg salad sandwich, will you? Before you meet Helen? Whole wheat."

She came to where he sat and leaned down and kissed him on the mouth. "Love ya," she said. "You're a sweet boy… But you smell."

He took a shower after she left, then mixed himself a new drink. He knew he was an old fogey, but Kee-rist! $330 for a handbag? She was handing it out like a drunken sailor on shore leave. His grandfather didn't even own a wallet; just a coin purse — because he never carried any bills. And now?

Helen and her cat. The lady and her toy dog. Schroedinger and his imaginary cat. When he discovered that the quantum mechanics physicists had got to his many worlds before he had, he also discovered that they agreed, more or less, with his theory. But they wanted to explain how it worked, not being content to accept it on faith as he, a good Lutheran, did.

One part of their explanation was a thought problem involving a cat in a closed box — Schroedinger's cat. They put poison in this imaginary box that stood a 50-50 chance of being released and killing the imaginary cat, depending on when the half-life of a radioactive element in the box ticked over — a random event. You couldn't tell which had happened — you couldn't say whether Schroedinger's cat was dead or alive — until you opened the box. So far, so good — but the thing was, the quantum physicists said that until you opened the box, *nothing* had happened; the cat was neither dead *nor* alive.

Their other interpretation was that when you opened the box the universe split into two universes. In one was you and a live cat; in the other, was you and a dead cat — and never the twain would meet. But the neither-nor business in the box before it was opened bothered him.

He realized you were supposed to check common sense at the door, but Helen's cat under the porch, say, was either alive or it was dead. Or maybe it had gone elsewhere. *Something* had happened to Helen's cat. If not, maybe right now I'm not here. Maybe I'm in Chicago and Ruth is in Long Beach.

Last week she'd said she'd call him Thursday night at eleven-thirty (nine-thirty her time). She didn't call until three o'clock Friday morning. "So what were you doing?" he asked her.

"I don't remember." Her tone was sullen.

"You don't remember?"

"No.... Barry? I think people did things to me when I was passed out at those cheap motels."

"What cheap motels?"

"You know.... I was doping back then.... You know."

He didn't know. She sounded as if she were doping right now. He asked again, "What were you doing tonight?"

"I was busy."

"At what?"

"That's my business," she said.

He hung up the phone with the pronounced feeling that if he went to Las Vegas, the trip would be a catastrophe. The next day he called to cancel but when they told him he wouldn't get a refund he let his reservation stand — what the hell — and here he was, wasn't he, all 13 buttons still secure? Twelve, anyhow.

He was tired and he was hungry and he'd definitely had too much to drink, Ruth could vouch for that. For all he knew, in spite of her moods, and her volatility — and her habit — Ruth might very well prove as exciting to live with as recharging a Water Pik toothbrush. Of course he might, too. Probably would. But $330 for a handbag? He charged his clients $300 an hour, but even so....

Men bragged they'd never paid for it, didn't *have* to pay for it, never would pay for it. They paid. But still, she was a good kid. Mid-forty and she was still a kid, a good kid. And people should look after kids, shouldn't they? ...Damn, he said to himself, this booze is mellowing me out. Someone to watch over her, huh?

He rose and went to the kitchen. He made himself a new drink but then decided not to drink it. He went to the bed, lay down on it, thought about watching TV. Thing is, he thought, we fear women because they understand us. They know that no matter how old we are, we never grow up either. Never. He closed his eyes. Behind his eyelids everything was red, a light, pinkish red. Maybe he was better as a brother than the other, he thought. He slept.

◆

All of his men friends and all of his girl friends — all of them from way, way back — were at the party in his mansion. Ruth was there, too, tall and beautiful, and there was a long, long table with all kinds of good food on it. Ruth was shouting to the crowd, "Hey, everybody! I don't even own a car! I'm from Chicago! Y'all *hear*?" But there were pieces of sharp metal all over the floor and he kept slipping on them and falling down and cutting himself. Nobody else was falling down. He went around the room picking up the metal and cutting himself some more. He cut himself and it hurt but he didn't bleed. It was like a big family party, everyone friendly, but he kept falling down and cutting himself.

He woke up. It was dark outside. He turned on the bedside lamp. On the table next to the lamp stand, atop the heavy, glass ash tray, was a white paper bag and a note:

72

He went to the bathroom and washed his face with cold water.
he went to the kitchen and chug-a-lugged the drink he'd made
before falling asleep. Then he left the room and went down to the
Superior's small bar and ordered a double Manhattan. There was
only one other drinker at the bar. Barry asked the bartender what
time it was. "Half past eleven," the bartender said. Apparently the
bartender was bored, because he started a conversation. He asked
Barry how he liked Las Vegas. Barry said he liked it fine.

"Great climate," the bartender said. "We've got everything
here," then proceeded to prove this statement by telling Barry
about a Ralph Somebody-or-other, the proprietor at the Imperial
Palace, who was a great admirer of Adolf Hitler, and who had once
thrown a birthday party for Adolf Hitler — in '89 maybe it was —
had his private suite at the Imperial decorated with swastikas and
floor-to-ceiling portraits of the top Nazis. "Largest hotels in the
world right here," the bartender said. "Fastest growing city in the
country. We got everything." Hitler's 100th birthday.

"Sodom and Gomorrah by me," Barry said, finishing his
second double. "You ain't got shit," and slid off the stool and
walked through the large, thronged casino to the courtyard outside and back to their room. The bartender's Hitler-lover story
was even more depressing than the dollar-drenched saga of
Shadow Creek. Fucking mindless krauts.

He made a drink and sat down in the chair beside the bed. He
reached for the white bag and took out the sandwich. He remembered the street vendor in Chicago who tried to sell him the
homeless persons' newspaper, *Streetwise*, and when he said he
had this week's edition the guy said, "God bless you."

That same afternoon a man with no leg below his left knee
shook a cup at him. He put a dollar bill in the cup and the man
said, "God bless you, sir." He was twice blessed within an hour,
that day. But he still had memory and responsibility.

He had hit a clear space in his drinking. Maybe it was the effect
of the sandwich. But a clear space usually preceded his getting
very drunk. He would have to be careful. He remembered a

blizzard in Chicago and walking in the street down Montrose toward his building at mid-morning the next day. An ambulance drove slowly past him and stopped in front of the redneck tavern built below street level. The driver came around to the back door and opened it and an old geezer in a white hospital gown tied loosely at the back over his nakedness hopped out, jumped over the snow piled at the curb, and scurried into the tavern. Now *there* was a man you had to admire his dedication.

The Italian priest, chaplain to the hospital on Montrose, had retired last year and gone back to Italy to live his last years in his native village. He said his pension wouldn't support him in Chicago. You'd think God would do something about that. Barry had often thought about returning to Minneapolis when he retired — but he didn't think he'd ever retire. He only worked half-days, anyway: six to six. Ha-ha.

He was finishing his third drink in the room when Ruth returned. She came to him and leaned over him. "Barry-darling, you showered!" she said gleefully. *"You taught me precious secrets,"* she sang softly in his ear. "Dum-de-dum, I got Georgia on my mind. You missed a good one, Barry. It was like being in church, with Ray Charles the preacher."

"Most preachers don't wear tuxedos," he said.

She backed away. "Not in a good mood?"

"No. I guess I'm still cranky from the nap. I'm sorry. Fix yourself a drink. Only drunks drink alone."

"Well...?" She shook a finger at him and sat down primly on the edge of the bed. "Maybe later. Helen is in love with my handbag," she said. "I think she's jealous she didn't see you first. We had the best meal, and it wasn't expensive. But we blew the rest playing poker."

"You and Helen sat in on a poker game?"

"Not table poker. Slot machine poker. It's fun.... Barry, remember when we went to see Gladys Knight and the Pips in Indiana? Merrillville? That was fun, wasn't it.... Barry, remember when you asked me why I never got married? What about you?" When he didn't answer, she repeated the question.

"Never met the right woman," he said.

"Before me, that is. Not before me, you didn't. Right?"

"That's right. Tell you the truth, I hate to say it, but I thought being married would be boring."

"Boring! Dear God, help us."

"Ruth, remember asking — no, telling me I was never up against it? In the cab?" ...Barbara Mitchell would be over 70 now, he thought. He had wanted to marry her.

"Did I say that to you?"

"One time I was up against it." ...Maybe she was dead by now, he thought.

"When were you ever?"

"When I was in the Navy." ...He shuddered at the thought of Barbara Mitchell dead, as if someone had walked over his grave.

"That was a hundred years ago."

"It only seems that long. I was light heavyweight champion of the base so I retired to play a little baseball and pursue a new career as a seaman baker, and to do some serious beer drinking. I was 18 years old and I could do anything."

"Why don't you stop drinking now, so we can talk? You said you wanted to talk. Let's talk."

"We are talking. The base commander wanted me to challenge for the fleet championship. 'I'm retired, sir,' I said. 'That guy'd kill me. I can't do that.' 'Terveer,' the commander says, me standing at attention. 'I think you should reconsider.' "

"I thought you liked to fight."

"Not if I was going to get coldcocked. This guy was instant doom. I'd seen him train. Damn near popped the seams on the big bag. Boulevard of broken dreams for me."

"*Light* heavyweight? Barry? How big is that?"

"Hundred seventy-five. That's the limit."

"You weigh a lot more than that."

"This was then. I'm standing in my corner, waiting, and I'm so scared I'm damn near watering my cup. My mouth was so dry I couldn't swallow. And here he comes, this huge big black son-of-a-bitch, everybody cheering for the bastard, 18 straight knockouts, undefeated. Oh, I forgot to tell you: He didn't like Whitey, either. Nobody knows de trouble I'se seen, Ruthie."

Barry stood and went into the kitchen, made himself a drink, sipped it, stood there smiling to himself.

"Well?" she called. "Did he hurt you?"

Barry walked back into the room, sat down in the chair close to the bed, close to her. "Never laid a glove on me. Maybe in some other universe I get killed, but in this one I wind up champion of the fleet."

"You said he was so good."

"He was. Here he comes, tromping down the aisle like a stud Percheron, pounding his gloves together, foaming at the mouth, damn near, and *whoops*, my dear, down he goes. Stepped on a bottle in the aisle and by God if he didn't break his ankle. Had to forfeit. Made the base commander pretty happy, I'll tell you. I was in favor of shooting the son of a bitch, since he had a broken leg, but they wouldn't listen to me. You know what that proves, don't you, Ruth?"

"I wish we'd known each other then, Barry."

"It proves that it's a whole helluva lot better to be born lucky than good. Did Helen find her cat?"

"*What?*"

"Did the cat ever come out? Helen's cat?"

"I don't know. I don't *care*! Helen, Helen, *Helen*! You came out here all this way so you could get drunk every day and worry about that bitch's stupid cat? She lives a provocatively dangerous life, Barry."

"Listen, Ruth, listen to me now. I'm not that drunk. It just seems that way. I have misgivings, sure. So do you. But I want you to listen. You remember when you wrote me you were in controlled psych housing wearing an orange vest? That's for potential suicides, isn't it?"

"What are we talking about now?"

"Goddam it, Ruth, you're a strong person. *Be* strong. Snap out of it. It's past time to find the right groove again and be somebody of your own again. For *you* to take control of your life again."

"Are you talking about dope?"

"I'm talking about everything. I admire you. I always have. You've got guts. I want you to succeed in life on *your* terms. But you have to learn to compromise with the rest of the world, once in a while, no matter how dumb the rules are."

"The rules are so dumb there'd be women sit out in the main yard and shoot up in broad daylight. And it was the COs bringing it in. But I had some good roomies."

"COs?"

"Correctional officers. Did you ever father any children, Barry?"

"Did I ever father any children?"

"Yes. You heard me. Didn't any of your girlfriends ever get pregnant?"

He shifted his position on the chair. "Once," he said.

"So what happened? Why didn't you marry her? That would have been the honorable thing."

"Marriage wasn't for me," he said, lowering his voice. "You know — the old story. Everything else was going pretty good, so why rock the boat?"

"Speak more distinctly. It scared you?"

"I said getting married would have upset the applecart. That's the way I was thinking then. Maybe I regret it."

"It would have been inconvenient for you."

"That's one way of putting it."

"So what happened — with your girlfriend, I mean?"

"She died."

"Giving birth? To your child? How awful."

"No. There was no child. She drowned. Norma drowned."

"She *drowned*?"

"Once she told me she was showering and what I'd done to her hit her and she just stood there crying until the water ran cold."

"But how did she drown?"

"She didn't take baths. She took showers. But they said the pump pulled in her hair and drowned her while she was taking a bath. It was a circulating bath. She had red hair, I tell you that?" He stood up and went to the kitchen and poured himself a dark drink. Norma's roommate had spit in his face.

Ruth called after him, "What did you do to her?"

"Nothing. Not that much. I told her to get an abortion." He came back and sat down in the chair again.

"Well — ?" Ruth said.

"I — what I did — oh, man, Ruth. I don't like to talk about this. Do we have to?"

"Yes, we have to."

"I went to her place and we had a showdown. She'd been on me a month — more. Phone calls every day at work, to my apartment all night, letters, baby clothes in the mail, and I said it had to stop. It was over. I was philosophical for her. I said sometimes one person liked the other more than the other did and when it was over it was over. No one was irreplaceable. 'That's sad,' she said. Not sad, I said, a fact of life. She said she wouldn't have the child alone. I said she had a pretty good start on it. She told me she would kill herself first. I said go ahead if that's what pleases you.

Do what you have to do. Do what you have to do, I said! And then I walked out — and she did what she had to do." He put his drink on the bedside table.

"Oh, Barry." …She waited and finally he spoke again.

"I don't like to walk out on people, Ruth, honest to God." He leaned forward, put his hands between his knees, began to rock, then shook himself and straightened up again. He would put it out of his mind, as he always had. He thought then: I know what Ruth wants and what I want… besides love. We want happiness and peace. We want our pain soothed, our loneliness eased. We want contentment and order. Who doesn't? But they couldn't give that to each other. They were too different. She must certainly realize that.

"Ruth," he said, "I've been thinking."

"I'm so sorry for her," Ruth said. "That poor woman."

"I know, I know, I *know*! …Ruth, it could really be that I'm not a very good candidate for marriage. The two of us living together would be one long battle, we're so different. You know that. At my age, I don't have a lot of patience."

She smiled, but she looked puzzled now, and wary.

"Every time somebody is rude to you," he said, "a little thing like that, or if I was, there'd be a battle. It's just the way you are. It's beyond your control." He picked up his drink and finished it.

She leaned forward on the bed, frowning — toward him. "What the fuck do you know about me?" she said, low-voiced and angry. "About my life? About what's beyond my control? I've been major-league stressed out the past few years. Major-league. You're a juicer but you're a white male and you can get away with it. I can't get away with *anything*. California's the most repressive state in this country. The only industry it's got is building prisons. That and junior colleges. Education and incarceration."

"I agree. But I also know I'm going on 64 and you're not, so I hope you'll give a little weight to my opinions."

"Such as? What I want to know is, do you want me to come live with you just for my sake, or what? To have control over me without marriage? Or as a *prelude* to marriage? I won't live with people without a band on my hand. Or just as a convenient piece of ass? Which? Or just as a friend? What? What do you want, Barry? I'm asking you." She stood up, began to stride between the TV set and the bed.

"Another drink," he said. He put his glass in her hand as she passed him and she clasped it reflexively and he stood up and followed her into the kitchen.

She said, "When Muffy got hyper I used to give her a teaspoon of whiskey in water. That calmed her down. Crushed baby aspirin would, too. You always have to control, don't you. 'Get me a drink, Ruth!' as if I were your servant."

"You know, Ruth, cats are like women: they're self-centered and they're stubborn. But they don't bark, you can say that for them." …Christ, he thought, she even dopes her cat. "I think I'd get more affection from Muffy in 20 seconds than I've gotten from you in three days," he said. "Really. That greeting at the airport, for instance."

"Barry, quit drinking."

"I'm not someone you want to father your child, Ruth. I'm a walking credit card. I'm an easy mark, that's all I am to you. A money tree."

"Don't get started, all right? You're making me angry." She thrust the drink at him.

"Okay, thanks." …Making her angry? What was he saying except the truth?

"You haven't yet told me what you want," she said.

"Right. Right. I wanted you to come to Chicago to see if we could live in the same place together without killing each other. A trial. So far I'd say this little get-together proves we can't. I don't want control over you, no."

"Yes, you do. Your whole life you've been manipulating people, managing them, getting them to do what you want. What *you* want."

"Have it your way. I just don't want you fucking me up when *you* run wild. I can swamp a boat all by my lonesome. Besides, someone has to have control. In everything. Someone has to call the shots. What's so bad about that? Sometimes *you* do, sometimes someone else. You tell me how you're gonna run a Navy, say, if nobody's in charge. You still got your post office box?"

"Yes."

"Answering service?"

"Yes. Why shouldn't I? Did you want me to drop off the face of the earth?"

"No, no, I just wondered." He raised his glass. "Here's to you, Ruth. May you live forever — and may I be there the day you die."

"It amazes me how you get away with it, Barry. The way you drink, you should be dead by now. Lucky is right. All *my* luck is bad. None of my dreams have ever come true. One thing after another falls apart. People don't keep promises, people run out on me. I'm not doing any of the things I aspired to, that I went to school for, that my mother slaved to get for me. *Slaved*. Still — I don't stay in a job for safety! If a job's no good, I'm gone. They can dog me, but I won't give it up. What I can't understand is, if the Lord won't help me, why does He have to help my enemies? The last prayer I say at nighttime, the last sentence, I say, 'Listen, Honey, don't you fuck me up, You hear?' And when I wake up, I say, 'Thank you.' I'm still Ruth, Barry, no matter how bad it gets, but it gets harder all the time. I have the courage of my convictions, Barry. I've held fast to the core of my being. I am who I say I am. I have ideals. I won't compromise them, coke or no coke. I strive to be a decent human being. To honor and protect others, that's the most important thing. But they won't let me be. I don't know why, the sons of bitches! You can't win! I'm not hurting *them*!"

"Okay, okay. You're entitled to be angry. If it was winning kept us going, we'd all be dead, Ruth. But with all due respect, Ruth, you bring a lot of it on yourself. You have a big mouth. No, no — I know, so do I. But you do coke, and I do booze, and *none* of it's a good combination. The half-life of any hookup we made would be about 30, 40 minutes, tops."

"You didn't hear a word I said, did you? You have no intention of getting married. You just wanted me here to put me through your hoops, like every other chickie you've strung along, like your girlfriend — the one who killed herself. And you're angry with me because I won't."

"That's a low blow. A *real* low blow, I'm not angry with you. I never have been. I never will be. *Never*. If I *am* angry, it's because I know you're smart, and what you've been doing the past five years comes up stupid... Ruth, *think*. You've got to set an objective, take *control* of your life. Then your dreams can come true." He knew he was talking to himself as much as to her, and so he forgave himself his pomposity.

"Oh, yeah — nice words," she said. "But bullshit words if I consider the source. You don't want to marry me, right?"

"I didn't say that. You hear me say that?"

"I hear a man backpedalling to save his life. I've heard it before. I recognize it. You're blowing me off."

"No. I'm trying to help. Ruth, get a picture in your mind of what you want your life to be like. *Think*. Then think of what you know you have to do — and, by now, not do — to make that happen. With all you've got going for you, you can make it happen. *Not* do, too. That's important. The dope."

"But without you is what you're saying."

"Not necessary. Not *necessarily*, I mean. I'm just a port in a storm for you. You think I like knowing that? If you get a decent job and back on your feet, it's bye-bye Barry. We both know that."

"Barry, you're such a hypocrite!" She was glaring at him.

"Don't get hostile," he said. "Don't freak out now."

"I'm not. I get intense. I get intense when there's something I feel strongly about. Others take it for hostility."

"Listen to me, Ruth. Listen to me."

"Oh, you're drunk. Why should I?"

He wanted to talk about truthfulness, fairness, loyalty, sharing, companionship. respect — love. He wanted them to come to an agreement, a rough agreement, at least, as to the terms they might possibly live with. If they could. Didn't he?

He remembered the 83-year-old who ran the bakery: "Without God, there is nothing," she'd say and cackle. And nobody believed in God anymore, or in love or compassion. So there was nothing, unless you made it yourself, was there.

He wanted to give Ruth love and kindness and devotion, all the good things that had been denied her. Right now he had a glimmer of such a life with her. The sun rises, we say — but it is really the earth spinning. First they piled boulder after boulder on her back. Then they blew the whistle on her for not being able to carry the weight.

He put his drink on the table, leaned forward to speak to her, tell her this, and slowly toppled head first out of the chair, his forehead scraping along the rug until he came to a stop full-length beside the bed.

◆

The drapes were drawn and bright sunlight flowed through the windows down on him. He could hear the shower running. His back was stiff and his left arm on which he lay was numb and he felt shaky. Lying there, he had the vague notion that there had been another big misunderstanding. With it came a premonition of dread that shivered and shook through his body.

He hoisted himself to his feet and went to the kitchen and for long, wracking minutes stood with his head over the sink, his arms braced on the counter, trying to throw up, retching with the dry heaves. The effort brought tears to his eyes but when it was over he felt better. Still jumpy, though. He made himself a drink, took it to the chair by the bed. Maybe last night would come back to him.

He went to the bathroom and rapped on the door.

"Just leave me alone!" she said.

He went back to his drink, sipped from it, went to a window, looked down into the courtyard at the trees, the fountains, the benches. Families and couples were walking below in the streaming sunlight.

He paced slowly back and forth in front of the windows. He stopped in front of the chair by the windows and looked down at his opened suitcase with his work in it.

After a long while she came out of the bathroom. She was wearing a short, white, terrycloth dressing robe. She sat down on the bed, her back against the headboard, her long, brown legs stretched in front of her. She lit a cigarette and looked at him through narrowed eyes. She blew out a stream of smoke. "Sleep well?" she asked, long fingers, long nails, holding her cigarette.

"You disappear into the bathroom for hours, how can we communicate?"

"We communicated. The message was: Why spoil a beautiful relationship with marriage? You're a jerk."

"Maybe a couple meatballs shy of a smorgasbord, yes. You cop from your little friend Helen? That account for the time out in the bathroom?"

"I took a shower. Last night Helen told me a 14-year-old got blown away in her house two months ago. Killed. A 14-year-old. That's Helen for you. You're welcome to her. You can't handle one, you twice as much can't handle two. You're a jerk, Terveer, A real jerk."

"Not a coke head, though."

"No, you're a wet brain. And who's a coke head? I do coke for relaxation. It relaxes me."

"You're ripped right now, aren't you."

"That first hit, it lights up your mind, they do say. I wouldn't know, 'deed I don't. After you passed out last night — oh, you've got a good-sized burn on your forehead, did you know that, Barry? From the rug, I suppose. That was a laugh, Barry. I had to laugh at you in spite of myself, you falling out of the chair like that, slow-motion."

"You were saying?"

"That I tried to figure out why you'd come all this way just to humiliate me. Blow me off. Not just a put-down. A rednecked, motherfucking cut-down. Want to do me a favor?"

"What is it?"

"When we leave here, let me take a couple of your credit cards back to Long Beach with me."

"Sure, nothing simpler. Can I sign over my household furnishings to you?"

"Just give me three days and then call in and report them stolen. Two days if it makes you feel safer. Five would be better for me."

"You must think I'm out of my mind."

She smiled. "Well, that, too," she said. "You up for that, Barry-dearest? Three days?"

"I don't think so."

"I'd show my appreciation, if that's what it takes. I'll paint your house. Don't be so cheap, okay?"

"When you get back to Long Beach are you going to look for work? You know, Ruth, I didn't blow you off last night. It's as much your call as mine. You rolled the dice, too."

"Why do you want me to get a job? You can't support me? You said you were going to support me. Didn't you say you were going to take care of me? What would I have to do? Eat one-half a piece of bread daily? Cook and clean and keep my 'big' mouth shut? I didn't know I'd have to work. I ain't gonna be no goddam maid."

"Everyone has to work."

She put the cigarette in the glass ashtray and closed her lips tightly and then closed her eyes and began to make a strange sound, like a stifled scream, barely audible at first but rising in pitch and volume until it peaked and suddenly ended. She opened her eyes.

After a moment he said, "The very thought of going to work does that to you?"

"I don't want to work."

"What do you want to do?"

"I want to vegetate and contemplate my navel."

"If there's any contemplating of your navel, I'll do it."

"Ooooh — that sounds interesting."

"Working would keep your mind occupied."

"I don't want my mind occupied. Nothing."

"What would you do all day?"

"I don't care. Whatever. That's *my* decision. I don't care."

"I guess you don't. Maybe I won't care either."

"You have to care. That's your job. If you do your job, Barry, I'll do mine. I'll be yours forever, if you'll have me. Or as long as you want me. As long as you can stand me. If you take care of me. Do you hear what I'm saying?"

"I can't afford you."

"What's that supposed to mean?"

"Maybe it means you'd cost more than you'd be worth. Ruth, how'd you like to be living in a sod hut on the prairie a hundred years ago, nobody else for miles around, six kids to raise and 160 acres to farm? People wouldn't be getting divorced every five minutes if they had to be together like that."

"Oh, wow! Barry Terveer, son of the pioneers. Big family man. You forgot the mule with those acres, Barry. That sod house sounds like indentured servitude to me. Is that your plan? You want me to be your indentured servant? That's serfdom. Would I have to pay you rent? Room and board? Work off my debt with sexual favors? That's disgusting to me that you're so cheap and petty, Barry. Don't you think that's cheap and ridiculous, what you're suggesting?"

She stood up from the bed. "Ridiculous," she said. "Cheap and disgusting." She strode across the room, turned into the closet alcove fronting the bathroom. He heard the bathroom door close, the lock click.

Short time between hits, he thought. He turned on the TV. The lyrics of a bouncy commercial were playing behind a montage of men, women, and children from all over the world, all of them smiling, smiling, smiling, happier than they'd ever been before in their lives: *"We're bringing you power, hour by hour, over the borderlines…. What are we doin' here? We bring good things to life."*

God does, too, he thought, though the commercial left the strong impression that General Electric was a tad better at the job. But, then, electricity, like God, was invisible, so who could really say?

What was ironic about this situation, he thought, is that her original complaint was legitimate, no matter what the watch commander concluded back there in Long Beach. One of the roads that had led the two of them here to this room began with the Arab motel manager overcharging her for use of her room phone. And last week the *Wall Street Journal* had had a long story documenting that U.S. hotels and motels routinely billed $4 to $5 for calls that cost their switchboard 50 to 75 cents; billed twice or more for the same call; billed for calls never made at all. The nation's furnishers of lodging had a billion-dollar-a-year ripoff going, a ripoff that led Ruth Harrison straight to Chowchilla when she complained.

He switched through the channels, watched about three minutes of a sitcom, five minutes of a game show in which screaming, smiling, mostly overweight women outfitted in strange costumes jumped up and down, clapped their hands, and tried with only fair success to answer questions.

He wished he could remember last night's conversation. Christ, he needed a break from this. Once, as guest of a client, he'd been far north in Canada and he'd taken a boat by himself one afternoon and gone to a little island. Lay there on a rock ledge for a couple of hours, watched the clouds forming above and move slowly along. Never felt so peaceful. Dozed off a couple times. Then he'd turned over and watched the loons. There were eight of them on the water below, four pairs talking up a blue streak. Loons had this strange, mournful cry that at dusk could nearly drive you to despair.

He felt a little despair now. Then he felt anger. "Hey!" he yelled. "Are you coming out of there today?"

No answer. Watch it, he told himself. Never make a decision, any decision, large or small, when you've been drinking. It would be too optimistic or too pessimistic. Either way, too rash. Never make a decision sobering up, either; it would be tainted with guilt and remorse, and unreliable.

Never try to work when you were drinking, either. You couldn't.... Which meant he better soon sober up.

In the meantime, there was this situation between them, if only he knew what it was. He pressed a knuckle to his teeth. The moments that shape your life for you, he thought, they ambush you. You can't foresee them, and you're never ready for them. In fact, sometimes you can't even figure out what it was you'd done to bring them on.

He smelled nail polish before he saw her and then she was back on the bed, sitting against the headboard as before. "Did I hear the television?" she asked.

"Half the sitcoms on TV now are all black actors, Ruth. Did you realize that?"

"I believe African-American is considered the more politically correct term today. Although I am black. Even though I'm not, strictly speaking." She giggled.

"Not African if you're from Jamaica," he said. "They stand there like posts, all in a row in front of a couch, acting the fool, ridiculing each other with one-liners. You think Paul Robeson would have played in a black sitcom? Not in twelve lifetimes."

"Barry," she said, "shut up."

"I guess they can't afford directors for black sitcoms to get the actors to do some moving around."

"The great thing about coke is," she said, "is it doesn't fuck you up. If you've got enough good blow, you don't have to drink. Ice water's fine." She was looking at him steadily, not taking her eyes from his face. "And no hangovers. No heaving once you're into it. I heard you at the sink. You're a real dirty dog, Terveer," she said. "But you're a nice doggie-dog, I guess. I guess. Nobody knows nobody, Barry. I can take care of myself." She lowered her eyes from his face, took up a small jar from the bedside table, and began to apply vaseline to her hands. She hadn't tied the robe and it had fallen open.

"If you can talk, you can sing, Ruth," he said. "Old saying from Africa, maybe you recognize it. If you can walk, you can dance. But rap music isn't singing, and it isn't dancing. It ain't even music. What's the occasion for the skin show?"

"Oh, blah, blah, blah, drink, drink, drink. If you can't fix it, fuck it, that right, Barry? You hear what I'm saying?" She reached up with both hands and eased the robe off her shoulders and sat there, fully exposed now. "I've got a treat for you, Barry," she said. "On Thanksgiving morning."

"I need a treat on Thanksgiving morning. What is it?"

"You're looking at it."

Her skin had a lustrous, golden-brown sheen. She smiled at him. "I have a love-hate relationship with men," she said. "Maybe you noticed. They love me, I hate them. Ha-ha."

"Intimating that you're not prone to argue? Is that the Columbian marching powder giving you orders?"

"I'm not even prone — yet. And I don't take orders"

Her breasts were large but not very full — somewhat flat even — but with large, dark nipple areas, the nipples darkest. She shook her head once, her wig hair flying against her high cheekbones and across her face, and then she tried to smile at him. "Hey, Pinktoes, wanna cop a feel?"

"Trick or treat?"

"Suit yourself, I'm an easy bitch." Her face, her hands, the slick, black hair at her vulva, her long legs, her feet, all of her parts were beautiful and she knew that. She slid down slowly from the headboard, spread herself slowly across the bed, opened her long legs slowly. Every gesture she made had its grace. At her gates, he thought, were the most pleasant fruits, ...and he was the dumb Swede lucky to be here this sunny morning.

"Barry," she said, "I love coke and it loves me. Do you know that? Do you love me? 'Cause once you go black, you know, you can never go back."

"I wouldn't know."

"Does that mean you were *cherry*? Uh-*huh*! That's a major league score for Ruthie Harrison.... Barry?"

"What?"

"Barry, I love coke and it loves me."

"You said that."

"I got me a boss high, Barry. Barry, you talk too much, you know? About dumb things. Okay?"

"I know. Same old same old."

"Barry, c'mere. Come to Ruthie. Ruthie needs you right now, Barry. Don't you wanna do Ruth? Don't you really wanna do Ruth?"

He'd been taking off his clothes as she twisted langorously on the bed. He tore open the small carton, took a packet from it and ripped it open and rolled a condom on himself and then he was beside her on the bed, caressing her, and her eyes closed and opened and closed and she began to moan at the back of her throat, her head thrown back against a pillow. He liked the smell of her and he put her hand on himself and in a few seconds more he was on top of her but he was so excited by then that just as he was going to enter her he came — quietly — and was almost immediately soft.

He rolled off and lay beside her. After a while he put his palm flat on her thigh. She moved away from him and he heard that same strange, muted sound she'd made earlier.

He eased himself off the bed, stood up, took one of her cigarettes and lit it. "Dishonorable discharge," he said.

"Just shut up with your stupid corny jokes."

"If you don't laugh, you cry," he said.

"You big stupid ox. What are you good for?"

"Fuck you, Ruth. Shut the fuck up. It happens."

She turned over on the bed and picked up the glass ash tray and hefted it, eyeing him with a cold malevolence. "Don't you ever tell me to shut the fuck up," she said.

"If you're thinking of throwing that," he said, "I should warn you it gives a wired jaw."

She put the ashtray down, pulled her robe around herself, sat up, and tied its cord, yanking it hard. "Sex don't prove a damn thing about love," she said. "Marriage is nothing more than civilized slavery, anyway." She looked at him again with malevolence, with hate. "Jackleg cocksuckers," she said.

The fingernails of her right hand were tapping on the bedside table. "That's the smallest dick I've ever seen," she said, smiling wickedly.

"People's teeth wear down, too, as they get older, Ruth. Why not their dicks?"

"That's how they tell how old horses are," she said dreamily.

"The size of their dicks?"

"We could have had such a lovely time," she said. "I thought I'd found a home, someone to take care of me, and then you reneged. You hurt me last night, Barry. You really hurt me." She put her hand to her mouth.

He pulled on his shorts and pants and a shirt. "Ruth," he said, "if it's any consolation, I was drunk last night." She would not meet his eyes now. "I was walking on my heels. I'm gonna finish off the bourbon," he said. He went to the kitchen. He looked up

and saw her get off the bed and pad toward the bathroom, her
shoulders slumped. Women always looked bigger in the ass, he
thought, walking away from you after sex with them.

♦

He sat down with his drink, took a wrapper off a cigar. No, her
ass was beautiful any time, he thought. It was that crack about his
dick that made him think what he did.

He remembered big, tough Cleve. When he was a freshman,
Cleve was a junior in high school — Theodore Roosevelt High
school — and *almost* made all-city guard that fall. The following
spring, one day in May, Cleve let it be known to a few friends that
he was bringing a girl up to his room after school. Cleve's parents
were attending a funeral in Wisconsin. Andy, the leader of the
half dozen or so Minnehaha Avenue boys that Barry hung around
with had been told of Cleve's intentions and so he brought his
younger followers to the alley back of Cleve's house.

As he sat smoking the cigar and thinking about Cleve and that
afternoon, Barry began to hum. He hummed the tune of "It's a long
way to Tipperary," though he couldn't remember much of it. ...Ruth
had told him just enough about last night so he could navigate.

All of them had stood there that sunny afternoon 50 years ago
looking dumbly up at the window of Cleve's bedroom, saying very
little, knowing Cleve was in there with a girl — but which girl?
Andy told them it was Eloise, from their grade. The shade was
pulled on Cleve's room's second-story window but that only
heightened the mystery of what the two inside were doing. He
and his buddies stood there silent — in awe.

Ruth came out of the bathroom. She was wearing stone-washed
jeans from The Gap and a blue-and-white-striped tee shirt from Hunt
& Peck; he remembered sending the clothes to her in anticipation of
her release from Chowchilla. She was barefooted, and supremo
attractive; no, better than that: She looked like a million dollars in
brand-new bills. But the expression on her face was stern, menacing.

"So, go your way," she said, "and I go where I go. But you've got
obligations."

He'd hoped she'd come out of the bathroom in a conciliatory
mood. He could handle that — maybe. "Okay, Ruth," he said.
"Okay."

"Fuck you, Terveer." She sat on the bed, against its headboard. "People should be happy with themselves," she said. "I'm happy with myself but I don't think you are."

"Not always. Or did you mean with you?"

"Because you're a fucking prick, anybody ever tell you that? You're a smart-ass, too."

"Lotsa times. They were right about half the time, but who gives a fiddley fuck? But while you're pissin' and moanin', here's one thing: I never came to you for anything."

"What are you talking about now?"

"That you came off pretty good in all this."

"Tell me about it. You're *such* a fucking hypocrite."

"You're into me for like 25 thousand and you talk like you're the wronged party. Bullshit."

"I never asked you for money."

"No? Anyway, tell me why I should buy you a ring. You for sale? You're a fucking con artist, Ruth."

She gasped and stood up quickly off the bed. She stood there a moment and then began to pace the room, exhaling long breaths, her eyes wild. "A con artist?" she said. "*Me*, a *con* artist? You fucking hypocrite." She grasped the handle of his open suitcase and in a single motion raised it above her head and spun on her toes and the papers and file folders in it flew about the room. "Who the fuck *you* calling a con artist?" she shouted.

The essential materials of a $30,000 report now lay scattered over the room. "You cheap fucker," she said, throwing the empty suitcase on the bed. "You *chingar* me and then say *I'm* a con artist." She shuddered once, giving him a long deadly look, then she turned and walked purposefully toward the bathroom, making the high-pitched noise in her throat, "Mmmmm, *mmmmm!*"

He sat down on the wooden stool by the pass-through to the kitchen. The phone was in front of him on the counter. She had him intimidated. No; he'd been intimidated in bed with her. What he was *now* was afraid of her. She would kill him in his sleep, or if he passed out. Take a knife to him while she was high on coke. And if he defended himself she'd call the cops and he'd wind up in a Vegas jail. That had happened to him in Chicago once and that horse was still running.

She had her plane ticket; let her get back to Long Beach without his further assistance.

He went to the closet alcove fronting the bathroom thinking to find her locked behind the bathroom door, and nearly tripped over her. She was lying against the bathroom door, her jeans open, stroking herself. She looked at him with half-closed eyes — but eyes that were filled with menace.

"Don't wear your finger out," he said.

He went back to the phone and called the front desk. "Would you send security up here, please," he said, and gave their room number. "There's some trouble."

"Nice try, but how stupid do you think I am?" she said loudly from the alcove. "I'm not falling for that. You're such a baby."

When the knock on the door came she said, "Hey, don't answer, Barry! I'm not decent." She struggled to her feet and tugged at the zipper on her jeans.

He stood at the door waiting for her, then opened the door. A man in the light brown uniform of the Inn's security force stood there. Good, Barry thought, he's black: a calming influence.

"What can I do for you?" the man asked. He looked about Barry's age, a little younger maybe. "I'm the security chief."

"Well," Barry said, "if this woman and I stay here together in this room much longer, I'm afraid somebody's going to get hurt."

"Woman? Where is she?"

Ruth stepped out of the alcove to face Barry. "You *called* them!" she shouted. "You *bastard*! You *did* call them!"

The security chief stepped across the threshold into their room. As he did, Ruth retreated back into the alcove, reappearing in a moment with her Evian water bottle. She tilted her head and took a mouthful from the bottle, quickly thrust her face close to Barry's, and spewed a full stream of water into his face.

The security chief stepped toward her. "You're in *my* house *now*, girl!" he said.

Ruth seemed to wilt. She had been raising the bottle to her mouth again but now she let her arm drop to her side, looked at the floor.

The security chief shook his head. "We'll put you in another room," he said to Barry. "You'll have to pay on this one, too."

Barry nodded. Then he went around the room slowly gathering the scattered and emptied file folders and what had been in them and his other loose papers and put them into the suitcase on the bed, finally closed that suitcase, and went to the closet and got the suitcase with his clothes.

Ruth would not meet his eyes as he passed her.

◆

Sitting in a chair in the new room, Barry was trying to decide whether to go to the bar and begin sorting out what had happened that morning or to the convenience store on the corner and buy a bottle. He did not know how to feel, what to feel.

One thing about throwing a binge here, as opposed to Chicago, he thought, trying to focus his mind on *something*, when you decide to come out of it here, at least there aren't 150 messages on the answering machine to remind you of opportunities you've missed, obligations you've let slide. Of course they'd be there waiting back in Chicago.

The phone rang and when he answered it a woman's voice identified itself as "Front desk" and asked if it would be convenient for him to see two Las Vegas city police. Jesus, he thought, if they moved my plate five inches, I'd starve; out of Ruth's frying pan into the arms of the Las Vegas law.

But when the police arrived — a man and a woman, white — they only wanted to know what had happened. Routine whenever there was a complaint, they told him. The security chief was with them.

Barry told them there had been a quarrel that escalated, culminating in Ruth's tossing the contents of one of his suitcases. He said that Ruth sometimes became intense if she felt strongly about something. He said his concern was that if she were to do something more and he tried to interfere, she might prefer charges against him.

The officers smiled sympathetically. The female officer asked if drugs had been involved.

"No. Just too much booze. Not her. Me."

They thanked him and said they'd go to see Ms. Harrison now, unless there was anything else he had to tell them.

He thought of something just as they reached the door: "One thing — she's a good kid. Go easy, huh?"

After they were gone he began the work of sorting the papers and file folders. His consultancy was the only order he had left in his life anymore, and Ruth had scattered this project quite effectively. Same for my life pretty much describes it, he said to himself.

He found the torn "Trojan-Enz" carton while he was working through the papers. There were illustrated directions on the inside of the carton: "…If condom doesn't unroll, it's on wrong. Throw it away. Start over with a new one."

"That right?" Barry said and tossed the carton into the wastebasket.

An uneasy feeling that he'd missed something, hadn't understood something, hadn't gotten a message he should have, was growing in his mind. As if there were an important factor he should have entered into the calculation but hadn't.

Still, he was lucky it was over; she sure as hell was no bigger bargain than he was. True? Hell, yes, true — she was damaged goods, what did he have to be broken up about? She was no young innocent. She'd been around the block. She'd worked in the entertainment industry. She knew motels.

But where were her high-rolling escorts when her address was Chowchilla and she was just another prisoner 90 days from the gate? Except to him.

He thought about all that and then he said aloud, with disgust in his voice, "For crissake, Terveer, where the hell do you get off?"

◆

After four hours of watching Thanksgiving Day football, he'd had enough. He began surfing channels and got lucky: the movie *Zulu* at the early point in the action where the maidens are shaking their little wooden spears that signify chastity. The Swedish preacher (who, oddly enough, spoke with a British accent) tells his daughter that "In Europe thousands of young women have arranged marriages with rich old men. Perhaps they" — by which he means the massed virgins — "are luckier. They are getting a brave man."

Barry watched the movie, fascinated as always, the fourth or fifth time he'd seen it. Every time he did he wanted to identify with the calm, laconic color sergeant who, when asked by one of the young soldiers why *they* had to die — as they surely would, 100 English trying to hold off 4,000 Zulus — considers the question carefully, then unemotionally replies, "Because we're here, lad — and nobody else — just us."

Barry would have liked to be seen by others like that — calm, in charge, no matter how desperate the situation — but he knew that for the last few days, at the least, he'd been the Swedish preacher, drunk out of his skull, worthless to anyone. The preacher's excuse were the 4,000 raging Zulus, but even trying to joke with himself about it, Barry could not equate Ruth Harrison with 4,000 raging Zulus.... 500 maybe.

He wondered what *Lives of a Bengal Lancer* was like. He'd never seen it. *Four Feathers*, yes, *Gunga Din* yes, *Treasure of the Sierra Madre*, yes, *Meet Me in Las Vegas*, with Cyd Charisse, yes... but no *Bengal Lancer*. No *Wee Willie Winkie*, either. Someplace he'd read that Shirley was dimpled depravity in that one. That must have been when Western civilization started going downhill, Barry thought: When Shirley Temple lost her innocence.

♦

He gathered his comb, wallet, and room key and left for the convenience store to buy a jug. But the clerk would not sell one to him. Somewhat flustered, he checked his reflection in the window glass of the store when he exited. He found he had to agree: He wouldn't sell liquor to himself either. It made him wonder what the security chief's and the city officers' evaluation of him had truly been. They'd seemed respectful enough.

He made his way back to the Superior Inn and went to the bar and ordered a double Manhattan. Over his second he thought back to the fight with Cleve when he was a sophomore and Cleve a senior. He'd always looked back on that fight as his coming of age, and right now his self-esteem needed a boost.

Since grade school there had been something about Cleve that he'd never liked, and that dislike continued even after Cleve became a neighborhood football hero. One fall night during an after-game dance in the gym at Roosevelt High, Cleve had called to him truculently, "What are *you* looking at, Terveer?" Cleve had been dancing with Eloise, dancing very close with her, and — not thinking about it — Barry had been watching them.

Instead of deferring to the football hero — and senior — and answering "Nothing" and moving off, Barry had said, "You," and from that, one word had led to another until they'd moved it outside, with an accompanying cluster of spectators. Barry's mouth was so dry his tongue stuck to the roof of his mouth as he walked out there.

He gave his suitcoat to Andy to hold. So did Cleve. He remembered thinking, here's where I get my clock cleaned, but Andy winked at him and he felt a little better, even though he was giving away 30 or 40 pounds. But he had done quite a lot of boxing by then, mostly in wintertime basement matches — avoiding support pillars, bouncing off furnaces — but still a lot of hours spent throwing punches and ducking them. His adrenaline had kicked in by then and when Cleve made his first rush he stepped to the side and chopped the bigger man behind the ear.

When Cleve turned to face him again Barry moved toward him, went in under a looping right and banged the bigger man in the gut twice and then stepped back and hit him in the face. He remembered the expression on Cleve's face: slightly puzzled; not worried, but puzzled.

The bigger man said, "C'mon," and motioned him in, Barry moved in and under and dug to the belly and then quickly out again, up on his toes, and clipped the bigger man in the face, then in under to the gut, back out and to the head — it became a sort of pattern.

His luck held even after the adrenaline rush subsided and after about two or three more exchanges, none of the bigger man's roundhouse swings landing, Cleve was showing signs of discouragement. When Barry cut the bigger man over the eye, Cleve backed off and said he had to play football next week so he would let Barry off this time. Andy stepped forward quickly and gave Cleve his coat.

The spectators accepted the outcome of the match with some surprise and much displeasure over its abrupt ending and returned to the dance floor in the gym. Andy came over holding Barry's coat out to him. "You did all right," he said.

"My hand hurts."

"Here," Andy said, holding out a cigar. "It came from one of Cleve's pockets."

Thinking back to that night and how pumped he'd felt, Barry ordered a third double. but even basking once more in that 50-year-old glow, he could not forget Michael Caine's last speech in *Zulu*. When the 4,000 warriors leave after their hill ridge salute to the valor of the British garrison, Caine is asked by a fellow officer how he feels after his first engagement. Surprisingly, Caine says he feels sick. "There's something else," he says then. "I feel ashamed."

"Goddam it," Barry said, because that's how *he* felt, after all, about what he'd set in motion that morning with his phone call to security. Shit, he thought: Loyalty and compassion — nothing else counted. And.... Jesus wept, he said to himself, and ordered another. And Moses slept.

♦

"Barry? This is Helen, remember? Ruth's friend? She said you two had a fight. Did you quarrel?"

"Yes."

"You're all right, aren't you? You sound funny."

"I might be a little drunk."

"Because I was thinking. I've got my car. I could come down there if you need anything. Ruth's my friend, but I hope you are, too. People have quarrels, Lord, don't I know it. They blow over. Is there anything I can do?"

"No. Has your cat turned up?"

"*Yes*! She was out in the neighborhood, I guess. Skinny as a rail. She seems frightened. Her ribs are showing. Are you sure? Are you sure you don't want me to come down?"

"Yes."

He put the phone back in its cradle. Yup, he thought, That's what friends are for.

Helen called again about an hour later, and he declined her aid and comfort again. Barry wondered, idly, what would happen if, after you took Schroedinger's cat out of the box, alive or dead, you returned the cat to it and closed it. Would the cat be neither alive nor dead again? Magnificat! 'S wonderful!

♦

Roughly every half hour throughout the night and into the next day, Barry returned to the bar for double Manhattans. He could find his way back to his room all right — he was on the ground floor close to the lobby — but early on he began to leave his door just slightly ajar, not locking it, because he distrusted his ability to locate the key-slot with the key.

Sitting at the bar on one of his forays, thinking about Cleve and Michael Caine and Ruth and others, and trying to make sensible connections, it came back to him what he'd felt standing in the alley behind Cleve's house half a century before. They all knew that some transaction was taking place behind that drawn shade up there. But he'd felt the transaction was unfair, one-sided, weighted all in Cleve's favor. Eloise was bust and hips and Swedish moon face under blonde hair and the only thing she'd been taught all her life was to say "Ya, sure," to men.... In a different way, it had been as one-sided between him and Ruth — and he had the advantage and she used the only weapons she had to redress the balance.

On another trek for his half-hour ration, sitting at the bar thinking deep thoughts — Is it important for us to be here? Is it necessary? — it came to him that it was simple: What he'd wanted all along out here in this gilded, glittering oasis was a translation to another universe and time where he and Ruth married, had children, maybe, but loved one another, and lived happily ever after. That was not possible, of course; it was a dream; but that's what he'd wanted. As his mother and father had had it.

What *was* possible, all that being lost, was to stay drunk and oblivious for as long as he could walk well enough to maintain a steady every-half-hour-or-so infusion. So that's what he did, knowing that life is the art of the possible — and that we are such stuff as dreams are made on.

He was eighty-sixed at the Superior for the dog-watch by the bartender who'd told him about the Vegas Nazi-lover, ostensibly because the bartender didn't want to "overserve" him. Barry knew the real reason was that he'd said that Las Vegas didn't have shit. "Supercilious bastard," Barry said as he crossed to the Continental, a block away.

For that bartender's four hours Barry took his custom to the Continental Casino's bar, which was opposite the Superior Inn. To get there, he had to cross six lanes of traffic. There was a traffic light, of course, but it was a wide stretch, and on one trip Barry considered walking against the light just to see what his luck was. In the middle of the night the traffic zipped right along and he knew that there was a high probability he would be nailed by a car, especially given his by-now labored, lurching locomotion.

Standing there, however, waiting for the light to change but considering using the light as it was, he finally decided against it; his drinking would kill him soon enough as it was, so why bother? His liver must be shot by now, why rush things? Why upset people? "Conscience doth make cowards of us all," a view elaborated on by Martin Luther, Barry remembered, as "Justice is temporary, conscience is eternal." …The agenbyte of inwyt. And they say alcohol destroys brain cells, he thought, erodes memory — *ha!*

Awash in a sea of sweet vermouth, bitters, and bourbon, the last he remembered was lying back on his bed and trying to sing himself softly to sleep with *"You say po-tay-toe, and I say po-tah-toe, You say to-may-toe, and I say to-mah-toe, Let's call the whole thing off!"* 'S marvelous.

♦

He woke to a banging on the door. He looked out the windows. The sun was up. It could be any time of day. He was groggy and when he got off the bed he found he had great difficulty working his leg joints, so he stopped half-way to the door. "It's okay," he said, "the room's fine," thinking it was the maid, but the banging continued so he went to the door and opened it: Jesus.

"*Que pasa?*" Barry said as the young Mexican came into the room.

Jesus stared at him with an expression equal parts hostility and contempt. He said, "Give me her two credit cards you owe her."

"Ruth? I don't owe her any credit cards, …If I did, you wouldn't get them."

"They are hers, Bar-ree. You have them. Not too tough."

"*Incorrecto.* She's hallucinating."

"You could have an accident if you don't. Fall out of the window."

"You watch a lot of TV, Chico? We're at ground level. It's like Joe Louis said, you know. You know what Joe Louis said?"

"Choe Louis?"

"Some kid heavyweight he was training — Ernie Terrell, I think — gave him some lip and Joe said, 'I've gone back, but I haven't gone back that far.'"

Jesus looked at him stolidly. I'm finally over the brink, Barry thought; I can barely move and I'm threatening this kid.

Jesus said, "Get the cards for her now."

"I had a good horse in yesterday's fifth, Chico. Real good. Took 12 other horses to beat him…. Not funny? No big smiles today? No jokes?"

"It's not time for making jokes. I'm not Chico. Are you getting them?"

"Not on your life, you fucking pimp. I've gone back, but not that far."

"You better watch yourself."

"Get the fuck out of here, greaser."

After maybe half a minute of menacing glare, Jesus finally turned toward the door and started to walk away in a slow, rolling swagger.

"Just a minute," Barry said. *"Un momento."* He got a pack of playing cards and made his way painfully across the room to Jesus. "Here," he said, "give her these. Tell her Bar-ree doesn't think she's playing with a full deck right now. Got that, pachuco?"

The young man took the cards, scowled, shook his head, and left. Barry turned back toward the bed. *"No mas,"* he said. He shuffled to the bed and lay down on it and eventually he slept. It was dark when he woke up and he didn't know what time it was but he did know that his binge was ended.

◆

"Barry? This is Helen. Are you all right?"

"Sure."

"Ruth's here. She's in a state, but she wants to talk to you. Will you talk to her? I think she's wigging out. Can you handle that?"

"What's she doing at your place?"

"She's staying with me — temporarily. Will you talk to her?"

He heard the two women exchange comments, then Ruth came on the line. "I'm finished," she said. "I'm fed up. I've had it. I'm through with being abused for $20 worth of dope. You planned to abandon me. You had no intentions of marrying me. I'm telling you what I know. Giving those cops that phony bullshit about your being scared. You big ox! Scared of what? Are you quite finished with your viciousness? I behaved at your behest. Did you ever ask what *my* motivation was? Your great scheme to ruin me failed. You're so sick and twisted and bitter and vicious you planned the whole thing, that's the point. Do you understand what I'm saying?"

"That you're having an attack of paranoia?"

"It was wrong, the manner in which you behaved. And making inappropriate, mean statements to the police, that was totally wrong. About my character. I would *never* talk about you to anyone else. They thought you were a jerk. They told me you were a jerk. They respected me."

"They agreed with me down here, too. What else is new?"

"It takes two to tango, Barry, it takes two to tango. I say what I want. I don't con people. I *never* con people. You said I was a *con artist*! Don't lie to me, you did, didn't you."

"Ruth, the gravy train has stopped, if that's what this is about. I'm not paying any more of your bills. No more."

"If you're so angry with me, you could rise above that. I didn't put a gun to your head. It's only money."

"Which you don't have because it's up your nose."

"What are *you*? Nothing more than a drunk. Those cops said you were a goddam jerk. An absolute jerk. I was in control of myself. I wasn't a jerk. You were. You pulled me around and pushed me. You pushed at my hair. You ruined the whole thing. You're not going to leave *me* fucked. You planned the whole thing. We could have had a lovely time if you hadn't been drinking. It was a violent, vulgar thing to do."

"You're suffering from white line fever, Ruth."

"Oh, stop that bullshit! If you'd treated me as a woman to a man, as a human being, but not you. If you'd shown some respect. You didn't want a commitment. You didn't want a relationship. You don't have a leg to stand on. You came on to me as a fucking drunk, putrid and horrible. You ask too much."

"I asked you to keep your mouth shut at the Devonshire. That was about my only request."

"Mr. Numb Nuts at the Devonshire was a pussy, Barry. You could have kept that room. Who do you think you are? Who's going to cuddle up to someone who hasn't bathed in a week? Brushed his teeth? Slobbers? Who doesn't give a shit? I lost respect for you. I'd just like to know what your motivation was. I don't understand your thinking. Using dope is one thing. The greater sin is people like you taking advantage. Who do you think you are? Are you going to honor what you said you were going to do?"

"I told you, Ruth, you killed the goose that laid the golden eggs."

"You're so nasty and negative. You fucked me over, Barry. You were a pissy, pukey drunk. You *chingar* me, and — "

"Wait a minute," he said, interrupting. "What does that word mean? *Chingar*. Fucked over? You used that word the other day."

"You smelled. I don't know how I allowed you to touch me. Had you not been drunk, we'd have had a lovely time. You were pulling on me, laying all over me with your stinking self, slobbering on me. Your great scheme to ruin me. The final blow. I shouldn't have allowed you to touch me."

"Or give you money."

"I didn't murder anybody. You had the greater crime. You should rise above that. I didn't steal it. I didn't put a gun to your head. ...Are you listening to me?"

"Sure. Do I have a choice?"

"Always some stupid, corny remark. You have someone there with you, don't you. You have a hooker there. I hope for your sake she's good. You can shine your white ass on her."

"If she was good, she wouldn't be here."

"What?"

"Nothing. What do you want, Ruth? It sounds like the record's stuck."

She didn't answer. Finally, he said, "I'm hanging up. Jesus was here. Did you send him?"

"You've got a problem, Barry. You'll die a most horrible death if I have to do it myself. But I'll have it done. I've already started, you fuckin' limp dick. You can't buttfuck me!"

"You have everyone who turns on you killed, Ruth? You learn that from Giuseppe? You're a fucking loose cannon, Ruth, you know it?"

"Oh, fuck, *bullshit*! There's no blame on my part. You're not going to leave *me* fucked. If I have any kind of problem in Long Beach," she said, "rest in peace, Barry, rest in peace."

"At my age," he said, "I'd welcome that."

♦

He sat on the bed, then on the chair, then one, then the other, back and forth, watching TV, not watching it. During the six o'clock news he walked stiff-legged into the bathroom, turned on the light, went to the sink, placed his hands on the rim and leaned forward.

If eyes are windows to the soul, he thought, then my soul's in need of some repair. He stared at the face in the mirror looking back at him, at the red, skinned patch on his forehead. For 25 years his face hadn't changed; it had been confident, responsive, serious — and then in just the last few years it had tightened up. He could still see intelligence in it, but now there was also the strain of trying for control, self-control, and failing to achieve it.

Legs don't work, stomach doesn't work, no appetite — all I need is one drink to get going again, he thought. Oh, yes, just one drink to get going again, all right. He had to get home, back to work, resume a normal life. Escape from Sin City. Lucky City, the Chamber of Commerce called it.

He was seeing spiraling filaments out of the corners of his eyes but he managed to look up the airline's telephone number and punch it in. He figured it would take him two more days to pull himself together. Three would be better, but he had a deadline to meet. With his ticket open in front of him, by an act of willed concentration, he got his departure changed to two days from now, wrote down the new date and time.

Someone at the door, knocking.

He made a tortured, stiff-legged journey across the rug to the door, Schroedinger's cat gamboling beside him, puzzled by the eccentricities of humans, their sorrows, their joys — none of those existent in an imaginary box.

Ruth stood there, dark and lovely. She held out her arms to him. "I'm sorry," she said. "I apologize, okay?"

He opened the door. A scowling Jesus stood there. In one hand he held a machete. A fucking machete, for crissake!

He opened the door. The security chief stood there with the two Las Vegas police officers. Helen was with them this time. He felt a stitch of panic.

Norma stood there, Norma with her red hair. "I forgive you," she said. She held their child in her arms. She held his daughter out to him! He —

He took a deep breath and let it out and opened the door. "Should I come back later?" the maid asked.

"Oh, no," he said. "The room's all right."

She smiled at him. He put his hand in his pocket and took a bill from it. "Here," he said, "you've been very patient."

She smiled again. "No problem," she said. "Do you need more towels?"

"No." Then he asked her, "Did you have a happy Thanksgiving?"

"Yes," she said. "My brother and his family came down from Seattle. We haven't seen them in ages. How was yours?"

"It was all right," he said. He shrugged. "The usual."

She smiled at him a third time. "God bless," she said and turned toward her cart. He closed the door.

I've got to get that ketchup up from the rug so she isn't stuck with it, he said to himself. He had come here seeking salvation. But did anybody besides himself really care? Does anybody know what time it is? Not in this town. He wanted to believe the trip had been worthwhile somehow — but he knew it hadn't been There had been no return to order; there had been no resolution.

The good Lord willing and the creek don't rise, I'll survive, he thought. Unless my luck deserts me. I've got the time. When he got back to Chicago, he'd — what? No sense kidding myself, he thought. When have I ever controlled myself? How many hundreds of times have I told myself to cool it, slow down? I've told myself that a thousand times, he thought. At least a thousand.

"You want to know what your trouble is?" he said aloud to himself. "You don't *listen*." He grinned, but he felt diminished. He felt lovesick and bereaved. Ruth, he thought, why did you turn on me? This, between us, was supposed to have been different for both of us. I was going to change your life in all kinds of ways — but, of course, one person can't do that for another. …The thing is, she probably saw that all he was really after was to take another hostage.

He'd gone with the drift again, and now he had the bitter salt of regret in his mouth. This was nearly the saddest failure of his life, right up there with what he had done to Norma. Close, anyway. No, he thought, you're coming off a binge; you can't make such judgments.

He went into the kitchen. He looked — and looked again — but there was no dried ketchup on the rug to scrub away. He thought a moment, then remembered: The ketchup had been on the rug at the Devonshire. His mind had turned to mush.

He glanced into the other room, at the suitcase with his work in it. Little by little he thought, little by little and all will be well. And all manner of things will be well.

The phone began to ring, startling him. He let it ring. I need some vitamin B-12, he thought; my nerves are shot to hell.

He knew exactly where he'd gone wrong, where he'd fucked up royally. If he hadn't been who he was, they could have hooked up. He wished he had tried, made his claim — done something right.

It was his fault. He was what she said he was: a hypocrite. It would have worked out. She would have come to love him. He would have come to love her. Maybe. It was worth trying. All he had had to do was to take what she was offering — and he hadn't. Not smart enough, not brave enough. You love who you think you love, that was true. But what if you wouldn't let yourself think you loved anyone? He had missed one goddam good last chance because he was too fucking chicken to risk it. Had been all his life. Again and again. A dumb fucking Swede.

The phone was still ringing — on and on. He let it ring. It kept ringing. Finally he answered it to silence it.

♦

"What could I do? You tell me. She's an abuser, just like I am. She's right on the edge. I told you about the 14-year-old got killed. Yesterday two of Jesus' friends came in and held a gun to her head and she was on her knees begging them not to shoot her. Today she started throwing things at me. What could I do? I called the police but when they got there, *Helen* filed charges on *me* — assault with a deadly weapon. That's a lie. All I did was hold up a broom to protect myself. I don't want *that* on my jacket, Barry. Will you help me? If *she'd* been black, they'd have taken *her* in, not me. I was their silent beef."

"Honest to God, Ruth, I wish there was some way — "

"Some *way*? Will you help me or not? Now *you're* deserting me."

"I wasn't finished. I just wish there was some way you could enjoy your little pleasures and still be safe and secure without winding up fucked over every time. Your luck is no good."

"Don't talk anymore, Barry, just listen. I'll have to do flat time, probably, because I'm on parole and she filed charges. ...*Barry*?"

"I'm listening."

"Will you come down? I'm in jail! *Please*. Will you help me? Please, Barry, will you? Do you hear me? Are you sober?"

"I'll take a shower and be down. I'll wear a shirt and a tie. That'll impress the hell out of them. A dressed-up hangover. Are you all right otherwise?"

"Yes. No. Barry? Don't hate me. Can you hear me?"

"Yes."

104

"What? What? I can't hear you. You'll be here?"

"See what can be done, yes."

"Barry, thank you…. Thank you for — well, Barry, for, you know."

"All part of our full-coverage service, Ruth."

After he put the phone down he sighed. If I can get my legs to take me, I will, he thought. Because it's a long, long way to Tipperary even when you're not coming off a binge. Right now he was the only one who could possibly help her, or might even want to, and he could barely walk. There's only one flamingo in the desert, Ruth, and it's pulled up lame and stove-up. He was here — and nobody else — just him, and just barely.

He wasn't quite sure what he *would* do. He knew that she was desperate, and he sympathized. But he also knew she had a tendency to bend the truth for persuasion's sake. And you could hone that tendency to expertise in prison; he had seen some of that here. He knew he wanted to believe her, and so as always he gave her the benefit of every doubt, and still he didn't know whether or not to believe her, whether or not he would go to help her. She either was defending herself against Helen or she wasn't; the cat was either alive or dead, but no matter which, Ruth courted disaster every day and, given her luck, it had caught up with her once again and she was once again a raging, middle-aged adolescent guest in the Graybar Hotel, her pretty ass in a sling once again.

The only thing he knew for sure was that he wanted an end to it for himself. Even if that meant hardening his heart and walking out on her to do it. There comes a time when you cut your losses.

He thought about Bugsy Siegel, *Benjamin* Siegel, who told the boys he'd bring in the Flamingo for $1 million. It came to $6 million, so they killed him. But before that, Virginia Hill, his girl, as well as the nation's greatest fellatiotrix, had squirreled away $2 million of that $6 in Swiss bank accounts, all unbeknownst to Bugsy. No. You couldn't trust them…. He thought about all of it.

He stayed in Vegas two days more, getting some work done, starting to eat again, function again, and then he caught his flight back to Chicago. He figured he had approached a destiny in Vegas, lifted again and flown on. He had tested his limits again and survived his folly, he thought. Maybe he was a little wiser for it, he thought. He had to learn sometime.

Schroedinger, the creator of the mathematics by which quantum physicists view the world, believed that the first postulate of quantum thinking had to be: "I am this whole universe." So do we all, most of us. The soul we seek to love is generally our own…. Is it not so?

The trip to the Las Vegas jail had been without incident, and Barry had done all that could be done. He got another deck of playing cards for his trouble.

But the end was still very far off, or might be, they both knew that. While we are quick with life, right up to the ultimate deep six, it always is. There is always possibility. That is what may be called the world's implicate order, and only the mind of God fully understands that. But though Barry Terveer and Ruth Harrison could not understand the workings of that implicate order, they felt it and its infinite interconnectedness. We all acknowledge it, do we not?

There is only this world, and what we can make of it in our lives. God does not roll dice. We do.